ENDORSEMENTS

Hector Vega lives out what he preaches. Having been through much pain and suffering, he has come out with a story to tell. This book is the story of the power of God, how it changed one man's life and how it can change yours as well. You will be moved, challenged and deeply encouraged.

— **Gary Wilkerson**
World Challenge Ministries

The Christian testimony genre has been done and redone; books of this sort have been written before, yet THIS story stands out—it's a story that needs to be told. Nothing can grab one's attention like a true story where the impossible literally takes place over and over again! Hector's story is gripping, tragic, redemptive, and miraculous. It's a story of a young man who went from career criminal to pastor . . . from delinquent to CEO . . . and from prison to praise.

— **Nicky Cruz**
Evangelist and Author, *Run Baby Run!*

Hector Vega's story and his commitment that others experience the chain-breaking freedom that comes only through Jesus Christ is a testimony to gratitude. This is the heart-rending but amazing story of a "five hundred denarii" Christian who knows that he has been forgiven much and is overflowing with a life changing gratitude and anointing that releases the power of Christ to set the captives free.

— **Rev. David P. Jones**
President & CEO, *The Bowery Mission*

A wild but honest true story. Hector's life story is so dysfunctional it stretches our imaginations. He lived a hyper addicted life that wound its way through the New York City world of Crack and Heroin. He was forever going in and out of prison until the impossible occurred, he was arrested by a different force. He was arrested by Grace......an amazing story!

— **Richard Galloway**
Founder, *New York City Relief*

Some people are unforgettable: their story, their experiences, their impact never leaves you. Hector Vega is that man and his story is that story that leaves your head shaking and your heart moved. I have know this man for years. You can listen to him and be amazed as I am.

— **Teresa Conlon**
President, *Summit International School of Ministry*

ARRESTED
by GRACE

ARRESTED *by* GRACE

The Testimony of Hector Vega

HECTOR VEGA

Foreword by
Carter Conlon

ARRESTED

by GRACE

Freiling Agency
www.Freiling.Agency
70 Main Street, Suite 23-MEC
Warrenton, VA 20186

Print ISBN: 978-0-578-40202-4

DEDICATION

To my heavenly father who loved me long before I knew him. Who deemed I was worth dying for, so he sent his son (Jesus) to die for me.

To my beautiful wife, who I love more than she will ever know, who stuck with me through thick and thin and was sent into my life as an angel in disguise. Who is still complaining that she only got one chapter in the book but without whom there would be no Arrested by Grace. She also says she changed my dress code so I should be more grateful! Lord help us

To my sons, Nicholas Josiah Seth, the arrows in my quiver who will be sent back into the enemies camp for Gods purpose and glory; each one strategically sent into my life as gifts from God and signs of his trust. You were the visible reasons I got up in the mornings day after day when temptation to go back to my old ways tried to creep in. Part of the reasons I wanted to do better and be better. You are my pride and joy.

To my precious, princess daughter Skyler, who has become our sunshine and a light that God has sovereignly placed in our family. Who wants to be my secretary and the drummer in my worship team. Who is already too grown, too old and too smart to be 4 years old. Lord help me!

To my mom who never felt she accomplished anything worth celebrating. Mom I celebrate you and I hope you celebrate this. I love you

To my dad (secret nick name Toey) who loved me and encouraged me to play baseball and coached my little league teams. Who taught me so much (even during the struggles) about life, hard work, commitment and loyalty. Dad you are one of the biggest reasons that I am who I am today. I love you.

To all the people who have encouraged me along the way and told me to run toward the light; who called out the plans and purpose God had for my life. The pastors and leaders who have mentored and spoken into my life. Teresa Delgado, Pastor Richie Weiss, Pastor Carter and Pastor Teresa Conlon, Pastor William Carroll, Elder Jerry Hampton, Elder John Hernandez, Elder Chuks, and Pastor David Wilkerson who started the church and preached the sermons that would play a pivotal role in my life after prison.

To my wonderful East Harlem Fellowship church family who deserve a special medal for still walking with me and enduring my sermons. Sweet Jesus! And Special thanks to all those who have contributed to the completing and publishing of this book (Sofie Alvarez, Tom Freiling, Melinda Ronn, Vacirca Vaughn and Tammy Shannon.)

—Rev Hector Vega

CONTENTS

FOREWORD

Miracles still happen . . .

They even occur in the darkest places of New York City.

That's what Hector Vega's life story, *Arrested by Grace,* is all about.

I have known and watched this author change over the years by the same free favor of God that initially brought him out of darkness and into the light of the Gospel. People who knew Hector in his dark days of addiction and prison would be dismayed seeing him leading and encouraging others to this same grace that radically transformed his life.

Let's just call it another miracle in the city that never sleeps!

This story will encourage you, especially if hopelessness seems to greet you (or someone you know) every day and laugh over your failures every night. But there is real hope -- a way out of captivity and despair! Jesus is THAT hope because He is THE way and calls to you, saying, *"I am the door. If anyone enters by me, he will be saved, and will go in and out and find pasture. The thief does not come except to steal, and to kill, and to destroy. I have come that they may have life and that they may have it more abundantly"* (John 10:9-10).

Hector Vega found the door and summoned the courage that is needed to surrender to the love of God. It was and is a different kind of surrender. There are no guns, no threats, and no commands to raise one's hands and face the wall! Yet, for many years of his life, it was the only surrender Hector had ever known. But then something happened. A soft, gentle voice spoke into the deepest recesses of his heart. "Give it all to me, Hector." It was the call that precedes every God-breathed miracle in this City. When he yielded, the Spirit of Almighty God came upon his entire being.

The promise of God is that old ways of thinking and doing things as well as learned patterns of captivity lose their hold when you heed the call of God. The man or woman who surrenders to God becomes a completely new person, living a new life in the power of Christ.

That's when the miracles begin . . .

You will be encouraged when you read this book. Perhaps you or someone you know will be the next New York Miracle . . . or American miracle! Because no matter where you live and who you are – God is whispering to you just like He did Hector. Perhaps, just perhaps, it will be the last time your 'mug shot' will appear in the police journals. Instead, you will now appear in God's book, called the ' book of life'.........under the title *Arrested by Grace!*

— **Carter Conlon**

INTRODUCTION

My name is Hector Vega. And this is my story.

You might be wondering why my story matters. After-all, I'm not famous; I'm not on the evening news; I'm not prominent – I'm just an ordinary guy. But I'm an ordinary guy who got entangled in a dark and chaotic world of drug abuse until I met an extraordinary God – a God who could (and would) turn my chaotic world upside down; or better said right side up?

It wasn't easy detailing all the sordid events of my life in this book. In fact, it was downright difficult, and sometimes embarrassing. I've never been a guy to care too much about what people think – but sharing all my humanness, or should I say, sinfulness, with the world was not easy. But it was necessary. It was necessary because my story shows the power of God and how He can radically transform a life – my life – and turn the chaos into purpose; the grief into joy.

I share my story for one reason . . .

If God can radically transform me – a drug addict who lived in immense darkness – He can transform you. You might be a drug addict (as I was) or a seemingly regular "Joe" or "Jane" who has hidden struggles – scars of abuse, failure, loneliness, depression, anxiety, rejection, or meaninglessness – but never-the-less needs a change; a change in thoughts, feelings, or behaviors. And maybe you are at a point where you feel hopeless; believing that there is no way you can crawl out of the hole you find yourself in.

But there is a way. And there is hope.

That's why I share my story with you now . . .

CHAPTER 1

NICO IS DEAD

I was awakened by the hurried sounds of correction officers rushing into the cellblock, key rings clanging together CO radios and — their loud clamoring voices interrogating the inmates. They were trying to find out if one or more of us had taunted or terrorized Jose in a way that caused him to commit suicide . . .

. . . a common occurrence at Rikers Island, a prison in New York City.

I didn't really know too much about Jose. Actually, I'm not entirely sure his first name was Jose. What I am sure about, however, is the fact that he had the same last name as mine and that he slept in the cell in front of mine. I didn't see him much since we were on lock down twenty-three hours a day, but what I remember most about inmate Vega was how depressed and withdrawn he was.

Interestingly, no matter how hard life in prison was, it troubled me that anyone could reach such depths of despair to cause them to commit suicide. And I couldn't stop thinking about *how* he took his own life. One inmate said that he had hung himself from the ceiling. Someone else said that he was able to tie his sheets to the bed and used his weight to choke himself as he lowered himself down to the floor.

Jose was a young man. Not much different than me. I was 18 years old and should have been doing something else with my life. I had so much potential, but due to my bad choices, I had little to show for it. And though my life was not peaches and cream, the thought of suicide never crossed my mind. Though I was a "tough" guy sitting in prison, I couldn't help but think what a tragedy it was for a young man to lose his life in such a tragic way. It actually bothered me – a lot. I couldn't get the finality of it all out of my mind.

On top of this sudden tragedy, there was another painful mishap taking place at the same time. Since Jose and I shared the same last name, the C76 Rikers' Island staff sent a prison chaplain to my family's home telling them that their son, Hector Vega, had committed suicide. Worse yet, there was no way for my family to verify the information. Due to the investigation regarding Jose's suicide, the guards had placed our cell block on lockdown. There were absolutely no calls and no visits. For a day and a half, my entire family thought that they had lost me to suicide.

At the time, I had no idea that there had been a mistake in identity. In fact, while all this was happening, I kept thinking about Jose and his family. How would they take the news of Jose's suicide? And I would mentally try to find that answer by asking myself how my own family would react had they learned I committed suicide.

According to what I heard years later, my family went through a day and a half of turmoil. My parents had started to prepare for my funeral – something that no parent ever expects (nor wants) to do. All kinds of emotions swept through my family – anger, confusion, depression and, yes, guilt. Even my neighborhood friends went into a crazed frenzy thinking I had committed suicide and was gone forever. While most were falling apart, my mother was the only one who refused to accept the news of my suicide. She could not believe that I would kill myself. In spite of what she had heard, and the circumstances that led me to prison to begin with, she kept denying the possibility. Many years later, when I finally discussed the incident with my mother, I found out that she told the prison chaplain that I was too full of life to ever kill myself. And she made it quite clear that she would not believe the news until she saw my body with her own eyes.

Ironically, there was even misinformation within my own cellblock. I had an uncle that was serving time in C76, right along with me. Evidently he had been under the same impression as the chaplain that it was *me* who committed suicide, not Jose. Since our cellblock was in lockdown mode during the police investigation, and we couldn't make any phone calls or speak to anyone, my uncle decided he would try to find out what happened to me. When he was able to visit the outside of my cellblock, he tried to reach me, but the guards stopped him. As soon as he could, my uncle came back to my cellblock a second time and began calling my name. He started whistling and calling, "Nico! Nico! Nico!"

I finally heard him calling out to me and yelled back, "I'm okay!" And it was through my uncle that my parents finally found out that it was not Hector Vega who had committed suicide.

My time in Rikers Island was difficult. It was during the hot summer months and I was feeling angry and isolated from the world. All I had to do day in and day out was think. And that brought nothing but despair. I thought about all my lost opportunities; and I mourned over my many regrets. I felt shame and guilt for being in prison – yet again. But I still didn't have the motivation to change – change myself and change my life.

No, I had not died that day in C76.

But I can say that I was definitely "dead" – even though I didn't know it at the time.

I was dead in my sins . . .

I was dead to my family . . .

I was dead to the ME I could have been without the drugs . . .

I was dead to society, locked away in a tiny, dark cell twenty-three hours a day . . .

I was dead to what society could offer me . . .

I was dead to everything God had for me . . .

To this day, I wonder about that mix up. I wonder if God was trying to show me what it *could* have been like for me—to end up dead in a jail cell, possibly from suicide or something worse.

You would think that being "dead" for a day would have changed me. You would think that finding out about my family's reaction to my "death" would have broken through the wall of stone that was covering my heart.

But it didn't.

After I served my time, I was back on the streets of Hell's Kitchen -- back on the drugs, and back in the lifestyle that led me to jail in the first place.

There was one change though. I decided it was time to move up, so to speak, to a better neighborhood; a neighborhood where people did not know about my lying and scheming ways. This time the drugs took me uptown to 137th Street and Broadway. I ended up in Washington Heights because I was looking for ways to get the most for my money. And I wanted to turn a bigger profit. So I set out to look for new drug partnerships in my new neighborhood. I looked for the big connections with Colombian, or Dominican sellers that could help me get the best quality product for the lowest cost. I was also looking for new avenues to develop street creds with the dealers so I could get product on credit before they got wind that I was a crack-head that got high on my own supply.

I had great expectations for my new digs, but my lifestyle seemed to always get the best of me. And hanging out in a new neighborhood didn't prevent me from being arrested again. One night, one of my Uncles was selling drugs in this area. I happened to greet him in the lobby of an apartment building on 602 West 137th Street. Unfortunately, we were unaware that he had just sold some drugs to an undercover police officer. As soon as I exited the building, undercover officers were all over me. It was as if I was in a movie--everything was surreal. I couldn't believe that I was being arrested for being part of a buy and bust drug sale. I had nothing to do with this. But since I had a rap sheet – and was in the system, it didn't seem to matter if I was innocent or not – I was always presumed guilty. This rampant injustice bothered me a lot because it was unfair and something that I encountered on more than one occasion in my life. For example, there was another time when a friend of mine saw me standing on 49th Street between 9th and 10th Avenues. He was driving a nice car and pulled over to the curb to talk to me. I finally jumped in the car so I could sit down and continue our conversation. Out of nowhere, several police officers surrounded us and then arrested us for stealing the car!

As was the case with some of my arrests, I went through the system and I was released on my own recognizance, promising to return to court while I tried to establish my innocence. I later found out that Angel had a customer who pawned his car to buy crack. Once the man came off his high, he called the police and said his car was stolen! The charge was finally dropped off my rap sheet, but my life had become a vicious cycle of drugs, arrests, and turmoil.

CHAPTER 2

⌖

GROWING UP
IN HELL'S KITCHEN

The old saying goes, "If you play with fire, you get burned." But if you were a young person growing up in Hell's Kitchen, New York City, there was no way of escaping the burn. Or so it seemed to me. Trouble always found me!

Hell's Kitchen, also known as Clinton and Midtown West, is a neighborhood in Manhattan, between West 34th and 59th Streets, spanning from 8th Avenue to the Hudson River. The neighborhood began with an influx of Irish immigrants in the late 1800s, and was soon followed by Eastern Europeans in the early 1900s. In the 1950s the area saw an influx of both Puerto Rican and Southern Black immigrants. On paper, Hell's Kitchen was known as a largely Irish-based area of dockworkers, slaughterhouses, factories, warehouses, lumberyards, and railroad yards that provided jobs to the huge lower-income immigrant population that settled there. But those who lived there knew it for its gangs, smugglers, prostitutes, racial tension, organized crime outfits, and drug dealers.

According to many history books, no one can pinpoint exactly how the area came to be known as Hell's Kitchen. In fact, there are so many stories regarding the origin of the name that it has made for some pretty impressive folklore. One popular story cites that two cops, a veteran and a rookie, were standing in the middle of a race riot near the corner of West 39th Street and 10th Avenue. The rookie took one look at the chaos and said, "This place is hell itself." The veteran laughed and countered by saying, "Hell is mild compared to this. This is Hell's Kitchen."

I grew up right in the heart of Hell's Kitchen. Not exactly the kind of place you would want to raise your family.

Mayhem ruled the streets in my neighborhood. On any one corner, you could find predators -- men on 8th Avenue that would manipulate and trap kids and sell them as sex slaves; women that lured you into a sexual snare; and drug dealers and loan sharks preying on the weak and the needy. Everyone was a hustler. Everyone had a scheme. You learned early on to keep your head on straight, your eyes opened, and your mouth shut. Minding your own business and being street smart, made all the difference between making it big and staying alive versus making it out in pieces.

In spite of all of the chaos on the streets, I'd always felt like I had it pretty good during my early childhood. We had a big and extended family— aunts, uncles, and cousins surrounded me and grandmothers who loved me. As a good Latin family they also loved parties. The parties were loud and went on all night, traditionally ending with a fight when someone had too much to drink. Of course, drinking was a favorite pastime at family parties. I grew up thinking this was normal and as a result, I started sneaking a sip of beer by the time I was eleven-years-old.

I grew up on West 47th Street, which was a little community within the community. In my mind it was the center of action in Midtown Manhattan running a close second was the old legendary 42nd street. There were at least fifty kids on the block. Everyone knew each other, and I always enjoyed the freedom I was granted to go out and play, whenever and wherever I wanted. Even though the two months off from school were short they always seemed heaven sent and long; it seemed like summer lasted forever because I left my house in the morning and came home late in the evening.

I grew up with a sense of adventure and mischief, which always seemed to get me into some kind of trouble. In fact, in Hell's Kitchen boys were troublemakers. We didn't have any boundaries; I can remember a pack of kids driving our big wheels, and roller-skating through the Port Authority just for fun. One of the kids in our neighborhood stole a bus from the Port Authority (just for fun) and packed the bus with kids from the junior high school and drove everyone to the beach. Stupid stuff for sure!

My dad was a taxi driver and a man with a hard work ethic. He took his obligation to provide for the family seriously, often working long hours and sometimes taking on a second job or various odd jobs to make ends meet. My mom was a perfect example of a housewife who cooked, cleaned, and took care of things around the house. She did her best to help us with our homework and we never questioned the fact that our parents loved us.

Life seemed good to me in the late 1970s but I was oblivious to the challenges our country was facing. The economy was weak and unemployment was high. I remember blackouts and long lines for gas. We were as stable as a family could be in Hell's Kitchen. I had friends, I had fun, and I had found America's favorite past time of baseball. I loved the sport so much that I slept with a bag of balls, my bat, and my glove every night. Of course, I fell in love with the Yankees, and never missed watching a game on television. I was a very skinny and short kid, but despite my size and seeming lack of strength, I was a pretty good baseball player. I could run, throw, hit for average and played a great center field -- and boy could I pitch. During that time, my dad took up the hobby of coaching my little league teams. We played in a league on the lower east side by Houston Street. We loved baseball, hot dogs, summer days, and the girls cheering us on! I would often dream of hitting the game winning home run or making a miraculous catch.

But somewhere along the line, things began to change. I began to realize that there was tension in my parents' relationship. My parents seemed to argue often and I didn't know what all the stress was about but it caused changes to take place -- including in my heart. I found peace in the streets and I was drawn more and more to them.

There are certain memories that stick with you forever. In my childhood one of my grandmothers—my dad's mom—was killed in a car accident. Her death really tore at the fabric of our family. It became evident that she was the glue that held that side of the family together, for as soon as she died; everything seemed to fall apart for my dad and his siblings. Shortly afterward, my favorite uncle named Monchie died of heroin overdose at the tender age of 25. He was found dead in the Wanaque Motel, which was a cesspool. I didn't know all of the details, but apparently he was a long time addict. He took some stuff that night that would cost him his life. Everyone was stunned by the sudden tragic loss. The funeral was painful and long and seemed to last about a week. I was clearly impacted by the loss.

My "happy childhood" took a turn for the worse and immersed me in the reality of what was known as Life on the streets of Hell's Kitchen.

My dad had always been one to hate drugs. He would counsel my uncles to stop using and selling but it always seemed like a futile exercise. Even after the death of my uncle, some of my other uncles continued in their drug addiction. At least my dad was serious in his hate for drugs. That is, until the early 1980s. Out of nowhere, my dad began to dabble with and sell drugs. Times were hard -- there were few jobs, inflation, and little opportunity. The seduction and benefits of easy money beckoned him so he turned to the streets for a way out. Looking back, my mother said she felt my dad was tired of working hard and seemingly getting nowhere in life – he took the path of fast money to support his family.

By that time I was already immersed in the street culture, experimenting beyond my years. At age eleven, I was already trying alcohol. By twelve, I was experimenting with marijuana, cutting school, and trying to be cool with the girls. Though my friends and I weren't looking for trouble, we often fought with other kids from other neighborhoods. We were still young and naïve -- we had not yet become involved with the drug culture that was rampant in The Kitchen but the fire was getting close. The street life was closing in.

And then everything changed very quickly.

What lures people into the drug culture? For my friends, me, and even my dad, it was the easy money. We started noticing how quickly the dealers made money and how they were living – they had the best clothes, the best toys, the best cars, and yes, all the cute girls. So my friends and I began selling drugs too.

In the beginning, the drug dealing was about making that money, getting the hot clothes, and impressing girls in the neighborhood. But predictably, it quickly became the way to support a growing addiction.

The freedom my parents gave me allowed me to go out and explore new things and to have the "fun" I was always chasing. At first glance, the streets are mesmerizing; they entice you, they excite you, and they seem to glitter like gold. When I would go out on a summer night, adrenaline would pulsate throughout my veins. I felt like I was ready for anything and invincible. I loved the action. I loved the adventure of not knowing what was going to happen one moment to the next. And I needed that excitement.

But deep down there was another feeling taking place in my heart. It was the desire for a happy home life once again; the stability of childhood innocence; the need for structure and discipline; and yes, the desire to do what was right. Yet, because I didn't know how to get all these things back into my life, I kept ignoring those nagging feelings and propelled myself head long into the street life and the drug culture.

Like a cruel taskmaster, the drugs caused me to abandon much of my conscience and to spiral me down into a life that pierced my very soul.

Eventually my dad started bringing his drug trade into the home. He predominately sold heroin. And though he had not started using the drug, he was certainly making a lot of money. There were all kinds of people venturing to our house at all hours of the day and night. My mother was opposed to it at first, but eventually found it hard to turn away from the easy money and the carefree lifestyle it provided. For the first time in a long while, my father was spending more time at home because he no longer had to work odd jobs to support us. Since I was already involved with the drugs on the street, I naturally started rationalizing that how we were living was normal and perfectly acceptable. After all, we weren't the only family in Hell's Kitchen trying to survive by whatever means we could. My brother, sisters, and I became immune to the lifestyle. I kept telling myself whatever I needed to in order to make everything seem normal in my head. The memory of these days and nights seem like a fog, distant memories running into each other. The sounds dance in my head. Things just moved way too fast and I felt like I was on a roller coaster spiraling down without the ability to jump off.

One night, as my dad, his partner, and I were in an apartment somewhere in the Bronx packing up bags of heroine [my dad paid me as his assistant in the family enterprise], my dad started to smoke freebase cocaine when his partner left the room. Even as he sat there, using the drugs right in front of me, I was in denial about it. I had already experimented with cocaine and I wanted to look away, but I already knew what the drugs could do to a person, so I sat there staring. I could smell the scent of the smoke and imagined what the taste would be like. My Dad looked at me and said, "Is this what you want? Do you want to get high?" I quietly mumbled, "Yes."

My dad looked at me and inexplicably handed me the pipe and blurted out "I think I am going to regret this for the rest of my life." I was only a teenager. I could feel my heart pounding in my chest. I instantly knew there was no turning back from this moment– not for me . . . and not for my father. And though I tried to deny it, I knew we had just crossed a line – a very important line.

I lifted my head and stared as my father spoke. Ironically, my father's words became a spoken prophecy upon both of our lives. I saw a lot of evil as a kid. Only the mercy of God kept me from and through some of the horrible situations that destroyed so many lives in my neighborhood.

The enemy of our souls comes to steal our identity; he comes to kill our purpose and to destroy our destiny. But there is one who has come to give us life, to make our crooked ways straight.

CHAPTER 3

PIPE DREAMS

From the very first moment I lit that pipe, my life changed. The very second I inhaled the smoke, colors exploded in my head. I became more focused and alert than I ever felt in my entire life. Even as the drugs flowed through my veins, my lungs—my entire system—my self-confidence flowed right along with it. Everything felt just... right. It was, in that moment, the best feeling I had ever experienced . . . but it didn't last. As quickly as the drug took me to the top of the world, it shot me back down.

And I immediately wanted that feeling again . . . and again. People who have smoked crack or freebase know the old saying well. One hit is too many and a thousand are never enough! You are chasing the dragon!

Freebase cocaine became the center of my life. It took control of each moment of every single day of my life. It became the motivation for my every thought, action, and reaction. I had to get that feeling again. I had to do whatever it took to get that first high back. It was the only thing I could think about; it was the only desire my body craved, and the only thing that could satisfy me.

I did whatever I felt I had to do to keep trying to get that feeling back. I stole, I hustled, I connived, and I manipulated my way through life so I could get my high. When I should have been in school, I was out in the neighborhood selling drugs to buy drugs. When selling drugs wasn't doing it, I started getting involved in petty crimes to get that high. I found myself doing things I had never done before; like stealing things from the kids in school and snatching people's gold chains off their necks. I even started stealing heroin from my father to sell and when I couldn't get my hands on that, I would sell fake drugs to people on the street. Whether it was baby powder or crushed aspirin, I would pass it off to people who were looking for cocaine or heroin. The whole process became an art form to me. I was proud that I could convince my "customers" that the baby powder and crushed aspirin were real. In fact, just to throw them off, I would put one piece of real stuff in the top of the crack bottles to camouflage the fake. That way, if they wanted to test it, they would get a real hit.

The Hell's Kitchen Hustler

Stealing and hustling became my way of life, a way to support my habit. People would come to my father's house looking for drugs, and I would take the money from them, (through a small crack in the door), lock the door, and then escape out the bathroom window. I was constantly hiding from my dad, who was always searching for me on the streets. I was too busy chasing that high to think about how I was bringing danger to my father and his house. As long as I got my drugs, all was right in my world. I did not care what happened. Looking back, I believe it was the mercy of God that kept tragedy from coming to my family or me. So many customers were upset that I had stolen their money or sold them fake heroin that could have hurt them when they shot into their veins. If it weren't for my dad cleaning up my messes, God only knows what could have happened.

Unfortunately, nothing was sacred – nothing was off limits.

Even my mother's possessions were not exempt from my grimy shenanigans. One day my sister Denise approached me with a cold look on her face. Her eyes were steely and she looked at me with disgust. She said, "What is wrong with you? Why are you doing these things? How can you steal from Mom and Pop?"

I knew my sister was heartbroken over what I had become and what I was doing with my life. I wish I could say that her words touched my heart, but they didn't. Even as my sister confronted me, all I could think about was getting back that high.

I not only stole from my own family, but also from my girlfriends at school. Sometimes, I would get one of my girlfriends to "loan" me a bracelet, a chain or any valuable jewelry. When I would say, "Let me wear that," they had no idea that I was on my way to the pawnshop for drug money. The family of one of my girlfriends figured out that I had pawned their daughter's bracelet for drug money. Her mom came to our house and confronted my dad with the situation. My dad came to the streets, found me and then forced me to confess where the bracelet was pawned. My dad was well known in the neighborhood and so he was able to convince them to return the bracelet and he paid what was owed. That walk back to the house was the most humiliating. I felt like I was walking the plank of a ship and about to jump off into the abyss. My dad was furious and was at his wits end not knowing what to do with me.

I felt ashamed that my father had to be the one to return what I stole from my girlfriend. What was even worse, this particular girl was my childhood sweetheart; we always had a thing for each other. Her mom had some choice words for me and she just looked at me with hurt in her eyes. I could hear what she wasn't saying -- She was confused and wondering what had happened to me. I felt horrible inside about what I had done but I didn't feel bad enough to make a change in my life.

As I think back, it's hard for me to remember the details of the early 80's; I was high so much of the time that many of my memories are lost. A lot of significant details of events that happened in my life are like shadows—I can "see" them, but they're not really clear. What I do remember was that my father seemed stressed out all the time. He was beginning to use heroin, and freebase became a habit for him. My mom was also on edge, which made things unbearable in the house.

My father and I were both drug addicts living under the same roof, and we were at war. There were constant battles between us and somewhere along the line I developed bitterness and hatred towards my dad.

As if things were not bad enough, I started experimenting with another drug called Bazooka. Bazooka was the residue from cocaine that was cooked in Colombia; after it was cooked, the residue would be scraped from the pot that was used to cook the cocaine. That residue was sprinkled on top of marijuana and smoked. It was a "go to" drug because it was like a speedball high – an upper and downer at the same time. Bazooka would still allow you to eat while high, unlike crack and in some ways cheaper than freebase cocaine. In those days cocaine was expensive -- $50 a pop for a half of gram and $350 for an eight ball. My friends and I first got a taste of Bazooka in one of my friend's parents' home. During the time I was hooked on Bazooka, I spent most of my time on 48th Street and 10th Avenue in Hell's Kitchen Park. The Bazooka business was booming and there were many Colombians and Ecuadorians selling the popular drug. As I became hooked on Bazooka, along with the freebase I was already using, things went from bad to worse. Once I started smoking it, I couldn't stop. I would start in the day and keep smoking for two or three days straight—without food, water, or sleep. I would keep smoking until my body finally gave in to exhaustion.

All of my drug use began to cause a great deal of conflict between my parents. My father had gotten fed up and would try to find ways to discipline me, while my mom tried to protect me from him. My father got desperate, not knowing how to handle me anymore. He was angry with me for the things I was doing, and maybe a little angry with himself. But looking back, I know he was frustrated and worried. He'd tried everything he could to protect me, in his own way, not knowing what would keep me safe. When he realized I was going to keep using, he told me to come to him instead of putting myself in danger on the street. Sometimes I would give in to the need for money and work with my dad but most of the time I would avoid the whole situation.

I would get paid $100 to $200 a night to package the drugs for my dad. I knew that he was trying to keep me close and off the streets, but I never got used to doing that work with him. Even after everything I had done to support my drug habit, I still had a sense, deep down inside, that I was doing something *wrong* in front of my dad and <u>with</u> my dad. Think about it -- who packages drugs with their father? I began to feel ashamed. Like Adam in the Garden of Eden, I tried to hide what I was doing from my father. Even though my father knew what was going on, I didn't want him to *see* what I was doing.

When I was packaging with him, the shame was palpable and somehow I knew the chains were being fastened on my hands but yet I didn't seem to know it. I was becoming a slave to it all and it took me further into a hole of depression.

During the early 1980's, Cubans started making their way into New York City from Florida. As we found out they were part of the mass exodus that Fidel Castro released from the Cuban jails. The Cubans were a different breed than Colombians, Puerto Ricans, and Dominicans etc....they were a little bit more ruthless and willing to do and succeed by any means necessary. They were here to make a statement -- as if they were hungry to make up for all the lost time in Cuba. I got along with a couple of them who just seemed to like hanging out with me. But what they really wanted was for me to give them my clientele and introduce them to people in the neighborhood. I did, but I always felt uneasy not knowing when or if things would change. I mean this is what life in the fast lane looks like; anything goes and anything can happen -- in an instant.

During this same time period there was a lot of prostitution, or I should say a new form of prostitution.

These were regular women -- moms, sisters, nurses, and secretaries caught up in the freebase and bazooka world. Women found it hard to say no to selling their bodies for a piece of crack because everything in their fiber is screaming for more; another hit please. They would come at me from cars, taxis, and everywhere. Some of these girls were executives who did things they would later regret.

What a scene it was -- people selling diamond rings, TV's, stereos, gold chains and everything they could find in order to buy drugs. If you had drugs you won. Freebase and later crack was powerful and "King" of the street.

I must confess, today I feel a sense of sadness at all of the women who got caught up in this whirlwind. Many are still in the grip of addiction but some made it out only to find that they are still in bondage to shame, guilt, and fear. They are broken and they are lonely while carrying a big, heavy load of regret and innocence lost.

But there is freedom in Christ -- He can break every chain and heal every pain. He can wash us clean and give us new life.

CHAPTER 4

DIVINE INTERVENTION – GLEN MILLS

It was 1986 and by now I was thoroughly in the grips and looking like a strung out zombie. My life was totally out of control. To give you an idea of how bad it was, I was arrested on Jan 4, Jan 7, April 5 and April 20 for different cases, in addition to being re- arrested on bench warrants on Feb 27, Mar 3 and April 21, 1986.

One day while walking down 47th street, I engaged a neighborhood kid in a conversation. It seemed like a typical day in the neighborhood but something was eerily quiet about it . . . Something ominous was in the air and I couldn't put my finger on it but I felt it.
Unbeknownst to us, there was a Federal task force called Operation Pressure Point assigned to Hell's Kitchen because of the epidemic of drugs.

They were on the prowl and an undercover cop approached us and asked if there was any crack. I said I didn't know but the cop proceeded to ask John, the kid I was talking to. I decided to leave and to walk up the block when out of nowhere, a taxicab filled with cops jumped the curb and they arrested me for selling crack. My head was spinning; it was another scene straight out of the movies. I was thinking, "What the hell is going on here. I have enough arrests in my life already and I don't need any extra help." I protested that I was not directly involved. Yet they took me to the 1st Precinct in Manhattan, and though I was only a minor, they put me in a cell with the adults. Their motto was arrest them and let the court sort it out. Never mind justice; arresting innocent people was fine.

The arrest with the Federal Task Force brought me to the big time. It was a federal case, which necessitated that I go to federal court where the stakes were higher. One day while at the Federal court building, waiting my turn in the courtroom, I suddenly got this feeling that I was going to be locked up that day and I had a panic attack. I asked to go to the bathroom with a plan in my head that I could escape out of the courthouse bathroom window. Even though I was at court, I was high and my anxiety was running amuck. As I approached the door to the restroom I stepped in and visualized my escape route. I realized, once inside, there might be no way out if I jumped out the window into the secure back area. Paranoid and freaking out, I came out the bathroom and glanced at the court officers in the lobby thinking somehow they knew what I was planning, so I changed direction and decided to exit the building as calmly as I could. The voices and pressure in my head were overwhelming. That's what crack does to you.

Once I made it outside, I ran to the nearest train station and jumped the turnstile. As soon as I was back in my neighborhood I ran to my base pipe. Ah, what a relief. I felt comforted. The authorities didn't come after me that day. In fact, it took them a few weeks before they caught up to me. But when they came – they came in force. They sent several plain-clothes officers who were part of a warrant task force. One car parked in the backyard of my first floor apartment on 47th street and one car parked in the front. They even had someone on the fire escape so that I was completely surrounded. The officers took me out in front of my Junior High School. I was barely clothed and I was humiliated as the kids in my school and my neighbors watched the officers put me in the car. Why wasn't I in school? The answer is because I was in the grips of denial and living in a mode of self-destruction.

Have you ever felt like your life is not turning out as you planned? That you are causing so much pain to those around you and nothing you do seems to work out? Yes, that was my life. I was making all the wrong decisions. After a while I started to dislike myself. So much so that, subconsciously, I wanted to inflict pain on myself to pay for what I was doing.

As I sat in the car, I wondered why so many officers were sent for me. It wasn't like I was a big-time drug dealer, or a serial killer. *I was just a lost kid strung out on drugs. I looked around at my school and some of my friends. It was then that it dawned on me that I was alone.*

They took me downtown and immediately put me before the judge to process and vacate the warrant. Once I was processed, I was transferred to County Jail in Newburgh, New York, and then on to a youth facility, in Pennsylvania, called Glen Mill Schools.

Little did I know that this was an opportunity to start over, but I couldn't see that God was working behind the scenes to help me leave the life of bondage that had me tight in its grip. I had a golden opportunity for a second chance. I had the spiritual equivalent of being born again but couldn't see it.

The warrant task force was the mechanism I needed to come to Glen Mill Schools. At Glen Mills, I was offered a chance to get my life back on track. It was a place, which used positive peer pressure and structured environment as a model for behavioral change. There were about 200 to 300 kids there from all around the US but there were only about 4 or 5 of us from NYC. We immediately achieved notoriety because the kids from NYC were usually sent there by the Feds, which meant that we had serious arrest cases. In fact, one kid was a bank robber from the Bronx. So, in order to one-up his crime, I started telling a story about my arrest, and before you know it the story had grown to me getting busted on a plane from Colombia.

I wonder why we feel the need to lie and embellish stuff. Does that ever happen to you? It's probably rooted in the fact that we don't know who we are – we don't understand our greater purpose in this world. We have no clue as to our true identity and so we make one up that seems cool, but we are never accepted for who we truly are because no one really knows the "real me".

Glen Mills resembled a college campus with a fraternity called the Bulls Club. We had a student council and I was chosen to become one of the leaders on the student council.

I was there for about a year and a half. It took me away from Hell's Kitchen, the drugs, the chaos, the gangs, and the crime; and in this place, I was able to think and act as a kid again. I got my GED and even played baseball again. In fact, I was doing so well with baseball that when the coach of a team from the Babe Ruth League in Pennsylvania saw me playing he asked my coaches if I could play for his team.

My two coaches were a source of great encouragement. Both had played in the major leagues

– Joe Miller had been with the Houston Astros and Al Minka had played with the Oakland A's. They were staff members and coaches at the school. They got permission for me to represent the state team as long as one of the counselors accompanied me to all practices and games.

Our team went on to win the championship for the Babe Ruth Regional League in Pennsylvania. We were then sent on to represent the state of Pennsylvania at the Northeast Regional Finals on Staten Island. The games were great with a lot of drama. In the final game, we played a team from Brooklyn with a bunch of Spanish kids. They yelled at our team and said, "Hey Vega, you should be on our team." We came within one out from winning the championship on Staten Island. It was a crushing defeat and most of the kids cried as we drove back to Pennsylvania.

The coaches told me that my time to leave Glen Mills was drawing near, but that they could get a baseball scholarship for me to play in a local division III school. They presented me with a great opportunity – a chance to further my education as an upper classman and keep playing baseball. It seemed like a wonderful plan. Unfortunately, the devil had a plan as well.

Part of reintegrating us back into home life included a weekend pass off and on. So one weekend I received a home pass and returned to New York City. The minute I got back to Manhattan, I immediately started craving the streets, the old friends, the old hangouts, and of course, the drug scene that came with it. What I did not realize at that time was that in order to follow the right path I had to change the decisions I was making when it came to the people, places, and things that I chose to be around.

After a year of being away it seemed that the streets had gotten even harder, but I didn't let that deter me. I went searching for the drugs as soon as I hit the streets. I went on another freebase binge and probably slept two hours during that entire weekend.

The Saturday night after returning home, I was standing in front of a store on West 47th and 9th Avenue and I happened to bump into my mom and dad. They took one look at my face and knew that I was high. I could feel the pain in my mom's heart.

Fidgeting around, I stood there, barely able to look my parents in their eyes. I felt like a big failure, a total loser. The only thing I could mutter was, "Don't worry, I'm going back tomorrow." I don't even think they responded. I knew they had been hoping that I was going to finally be free from all the drugs, chaos, and mayhem. I had hoped for that as well. Unfortunately, we were all wrong.

I went back to Glen Mills School and during practice was called straight into my coach's office. He took one look at my sunken face, and hollow cheeks, and gasped. "What the hell happened to you?" he barked. "How in the world did you lose so much weight in just two days? What were you doing? You look like you haven't slept since I last saw you!"

When I didn't answer, he got in my face and yelled, "You and I both know what you were up to. Look, Hector, you need to make a decision, and I mean now. Either you stay here, get your education, play ball, and make something of yourself, or you can go back to the city and die. If you go back there, it could be the end of all that you have accomplished." The problem with getting high after you have been clean is that it brings you back to square one. You have crossed the line and the drugs play tricks on your mind. Your addiction takes control.

By the time I was ready to leave the Glen Mills program, I was no longer focused on baseball, or a desire to do more with my life. All I cared about was getting back to the streets. Somehow, I thought it would be different. I told myself that I could beat this thing. I was lying to myself. Every argument in my head I justified with another argument. Looking back, it was one of those decisions I would always regret -- No matter how much success or distance from the mistake I have traveled.

The mentality of a drug addict is that you want to do the same thing over and over yet expecting a different result. That is why it is called insanity. I had success in my grasp at Glen Mills – how could I choose to go back to the streets? My decision was provoked by one weekend of getting high. That's all it took for me to be dragged back into the grips of the desire to return to my old lifestyle. I made the dumbest and most reckless decision of my life – in spite of all that I had going for me, and my coaches pleading for me to stay as an upperclassman. I finished my time at Glen Mills and was discharged on November 02, 1987. As soon as I was back on my turf, during the holidays, that fever started to heat up.

I really tried hard to stay clean but I was kidding myself. I was a slave being led by a cruel taskmaster . . .

Here we go again!

I limped along for two months but at the start of 1988. I was full swing into my drug-fueled life, which led to four new arrests (Jan 11, Jan 12, Feb 4, Feb 7). Wow! Did I really miss jail that much? Or did I really want to be free?

All of a sudden Glen Mills seemed like a better alternative, and now I was willing to go back as an upper classmen but they would not take me, and the courts refused to send me since it didn't seem to work the first time. I saw the stupidity and the error of my ways.

I continued to plead with the authorities to send me back to Glen Mills but that ship had sailed.

Roach is Free -- What about Me?

On March 30, I was arrested again and on May of 1988 I pled guilty and received a one-year sentence to be served at Rikers Island. I couldn't believe I was back inside a cell!

One night, a roach entered my cell and immediately I remembered a story about a man who was caught up in the cycle of drugs and prison. He kept hearing that he needed to change people, places and things. One day he decided to change his environment and he was successful for a short period of time but the problem was that he had changed his surroundings but not his way of thinking and behaving. He began to dabble with compromise here and there and before he knew what was happening, he found himself back in prison. He swore he would never return and yet here he was. One night, as he considered his situation, there was a roach that began to enter the cell under the door. The light was shining in the room and it seemed to magnify the roach like a spotlight. The roach took a few steps into the cell and seemed to be looking straight at him! Then, just like that, the roach did an about face and walked back out of the cell. And suddenly it hit him! He was a man created in God's image and likeness, destined for freedom and he was stuck in a cell. The lowly roach was free to come and go as it pleased but he could not.

During this particular time in Rikers Island I started to hear people talk about Jesus and how he could change a person's life. I'm afraid I didn't give it much thought at the time. Instead, I would go on to complete my one-year term, and taste freedom again at the end of 1988

CHAPTER 5

THE SHORT CUT
(180 DAYS AND WAKE UP!)

Like a rerun of a bad movie -- On Jan 3 and Feb 18, 1989 I was arrested two more times with two open drug charges.

Jail, was like my vacation home only, unlike other folks, it seemed I liked to stay longer than a week at a time. By this point the prison guard didn't need to assign me a jailhouse number they knew me by name.

The prosecutor offered me a plea bargain of 2.5 to 5 years and I jumped on it. Why did I keep getting chances to beat the system? Did someone want me to be free?

Since I was not a high-risk inmate, I was sent to a medium-security prison. I was granted an opportunity to get involved with a military program, which was popular in the prison system during that time because the jails were over-crowded and they were looking for a way to get non-violent criminals back on the streets. They created a military-style program that was run by correctional officers who either had a military background, or went through a short-term military-style training to manage the inmates.

This military-style program I was offered was called "The Shock Program."

I was told that if I could survive the humiliation, the taunting, and discipline that the correctional officers would put me through, then I could be home in one hundred and eighty days. Six months versus two and half years? What would any person in my position do? It wasn't a bad trade, from what I could see. I made up my mind to take a chance and complete the program. This was the fastest way home.

It didn't take long to see why it was called "The Shock Program." When I arrived, there were a little over fifty inmates, but by the end of the first few weeks, we were down about ten guys... and they kept dropping like flies.

We got up at the crack of dawn to go out into the bitter, Upstate New York cold weather [in our skimpy sweat suits] to run around and exercise. I learned to live in six-minute blocks of time. Every morning, we had six minutes to get up, shower, get dressed, use the restrooms, make our bed and get outside. And we had "six-minute time-outs," when we had to sit down without making any noise whatsoever. We were rounded up into the staff parking lots and drilled over and over with rigorous military exercises. Not even the cafeteria offered any solace. We had only six minutes to eat breakfast, lunch, and dinner. We'd have to stand at attention and remain silent while waiting single file in line. When it was my turn to get food I had to communicate what I wanted to eat, without saying one word, by using my hands as an indicator. Before we could have one bite of our food, we had to wait at the table in silence until the drill sergeant gave the signal to sit and eat. And we had to eat everything on our plate – whether we liked it or not! If you didn't eat all the food on your plate, the drill sergeants would stuff the food down into your pockets, down your shirt, in your underwear, or wherever they felt like putting it. I learned to take only what I would eat.

Our rooms had to be ready for inspection at all times. All of the beds had to be made to perfection; all shoes had to be shined and lined up perfectly under the bed; all the shirts had to be neatly placed in the locker, two fingers apart. We were only allowed six pairs of socks that had to be rolled in a specific way, and our pants had to be perfectly ironed with a sharp crease. Everything had to be perfect!

The "Shock Program" was all about discipline and repetition. We had to stay on schedule. Everything had a time limit to it. Even the Substance Abuse Treatment Program had a certain time limit each day. We had to learn to recite and memorize general orders. Every member of a platoon—your team—had to work together to learn all of the rules, regulations, and be accountable for one another

Community service was a big part of the "Shock Program" as well. We were taken into (predominantly) Caucasian towns to cleanup parks and pick-up trash on the side of the road in the bitter cold. We were asked to cleanup areas with big tree trunks with no heavy machinery. We ate in the cold -- sometimes hot dogs, while snowflakes fell. It was a bitter time and I hated it, but I kept telling myself 6 months and I am out. I can do anything for 6 months!

I held on and over time, I became a squad leader that eventually led to my becoming the platoon leader for my entire group. By the end of the program, about twenty-eight graduated out of a group of over fifty.

I learned a lot about myself at the "Shock Program", and I realized that I even had some leadership skills. The addiction program was modeled on the "Alcoholics Anonymous Twelve Step Program." I went to these groups and learned about drugs and what they do to our brains.

The military program had one agenda. It seemed like they made it their mission to break us so we would give up. They did things like the famous "Knucklehead Drill," where they took us outside to the middle of the field, right after lunch, where all the other platoons could see us. They made us do a bunch of mountain climbers, sit-ups, and push-ups; two hours of calisthenics before taking us to an area with mud and making us crawl through it. Then, as if to add insult to injury. We had to do the captains run (a five mile run, as fast as we could). No matter how hard you ran, if you stopped during one of the drills, you were asked to keep going or you got kicked out of the program and sent back to prison!

I did not give up! In fact, I was amazed that I was mentally capable of handling the structure and discipline of the program, especially considering the undisciplined life I had lived. I excelled in structure and enjoyed the military style program. I also learned how substance abuse affected my moods, my life, and my family. After learning these facts, I made a decision, in my heart, that I would not allow the commanding officers to break me, the drugs to destroy me, or society to label me. I told myself that I was not going to use again. Somehow, God was using this place to instill a certain fight in my character.

However, I needed to prove to myself that I would never use again on the streets where it counted.

A New Addiction

At first, when I came out of the Shock Program, I kept up my sobriety. I started attending NA meetings and I moved upstate to Syracuse, New York for a change of pace. I felt that I couldn't survive in my old neighborhood, but soon as I arrived in Syracuse I was bored out of my mind. I found it dreary and miserable. Although I didn't start getting high with drugs, I started getting restless. I decided to go back to New York City and I didn't use drugs for the next two plus years; I was working odd jobs at the Chelsea Piers, and the Jacob Javits Center. What I didn't do, though, was a problem. I didn't continue going to the NA or AA meetings; I didn't have a sponsor, and I didn't have a support system to keep me in check. Even though I tried to keep myself in line, somehow I knew it was only a matter of time. It was as if something was chasing me and I was running scared. Deep down inside, I didn't believe I would go very far or that I could succeed. I didn't realize that changing my environment did not mean the desires of my heart would change. I was still Nico -- I was still a bad day away from falling into the abyss again.

I initially found a replacement for my drug addiction. My newfound "drug of choice" was going out for some drinks and joining the club scene. I went to all the well-known clubs like Roseland, Latin Quarters, Bedrocks, The Palladium, and Roxy's. I focused my energy on pursuing women. It felt like I was living a normal life -- at least normal in comparison to what I had been doing in the past few years. I knew there was an invisible line that I couldn't cross, and if I crossed it, I would be gone. So I kept going to the clubs . . . I kept having a few drinks . . . This became my new addiction.

I seemed to be popular in the clubs because of my outgoing personality, and from time to time I was successful with the ladies. This gave me a sense of self-esteem that I never got with drugs. Deep down my life was still a mess; I didn't have a regular job, and emotionally I was still young. Never mind the fact that I still had not dealt with the root causes of my addiction or my sin for that matter. I ignored the deep longing in my heart. I continued to seek something new to fill it. I never dealt with the feelings of guilt I carried, for all the pain I caused, and the pain I suffered. Many of us never talk about or deal with the pain inside, so we try to self medicate and quiet the voice.

Nothing seemed to fill the void that was deep inside of me – not even the nights with beautiful women removed the gnawing feeling in the morning.

Then I met someone who changed the trajectory of my life.

CHAPTER 6

MICHELLE

I somehow sensed she was different than the other girls. She had style, grace . . . and she was beautiful.

Her name was Michelle. One day she showed up in my neighborhood with some of her friends. Michelle stood out to me. She dressed differently than the other girls -- cowboy boots and blue jean shorts. There was a sense of style about her that I had not seen with other girls in the neighborhood. I could not take my eyes off of her. I told my friends, Victor, Wilson, and Dazzy, that I was interested in her. Evidently they knew Michelle because they said, "Forget it. You don't have a chance with her – you're not her type; she's a church girl." I made a friendly bet with them and told them I would pursue her and succeed. But I didn't realize just how different this girl would turn out to be.

Michelle spent a lot of time playing hard to get; and even though I didn't approach her aggressively from the start, I did try to engage her attention. Early on, Michelle didn't give me the time of day. I learned, later on, that she knew a lot more about me than I ever imagined. Michelle had heard all about the kid who was on drugs, stealing, and always getting locked up. Michelle was 17 and I was 20, and she was not interested in any of my drama.

One night I saw her at a club named Bedrock's on 49th Street. In a move of boldness, I grabbed her hand and pulled her over to a booth to sit down and talk. Our conversation lasted quite some time and I finally got her to agree to go out with me. Michelle had a friend who was dating one of my friends, and she divulged to me that Michelle really liked me but would not let on. There was no doubt that Michelle was a challenge for me – but I loved that. As we got to know one another, I found out that she worked as a fitness instructor at Living Well Lady.

I started sending her little gifts and trinkets to let her know I was still interested. Sometimes I would get my little brother to take teddy bears to her. Michelle, on the other hand, kept playing coy with me. It seemed she wasn't as interested in me as I was in her. Though she was on my mind all the time, I started to back off and give her space. One day she came to me and said that she wanted me to know that I could see other people. I said, "If this is how you want it let's do it."

The next day Michelle came strolling down the neighborhood and just happened to see me chatting with a blonde who wasn't from the neighborhood. She tried to play it off as if she didn't see me but I was watching her, though I acted as if I didn't see her. Michelle glared at me until finally our eyes met. She approached and asked if we could have a word. I excused myself from the young lady and walked away with Michelle. She began to question me, flipping out, with a not-so-pretty language. I said "oh she's just a friend" (a friend was terminology that was very popular and double talk in our day, which meant maybe there was something more or maybe not). I started to laugh because she was furious; and I replied that I was seeing other people as she had requested. But Michelle flipped the definition of seeing other people on me. She told me that other people meant outside of the neighborhood -- not around Hell's Kitchen. Well, isn't this a blip! I never got the memo clarifying that.

Another Type of Drug – Quieting the Voice of Regret

While I was trying to slow down my efforts to capture Michelle's heart, I was also doing everything possible to stay away from crack. However, one of my friends told me about his dabbling with heroin and encouraged me to try it out. He assured me that heroin was far easier to get and didn't require as much use to achieve the feeling of euphoria that crack or freebase would give. I was always primarily a crack- cocaine user, but I had become terrified of using the drug after all that I had been through. As much as I hated to admit it, I missed the feeling of being high.

I had been selling heroin for quite some time. I encountered numerous people that shot the drug into their veins but it never really appealed to me. In fact my first encounter with using heroin was back on 47th Street at my family's home. My dad had an old stereo with a record (LP) on the wheel. On that wheel there was a massive mountain of beige powder. It was heroin in the process of being cut for multiplication. I decided I was going to sniff some and see what it felt like. What a huge mistake. My Aunt Lisa ended up finding me on the floor by the toilet vomiting. After that experience I was never drawn to it.

Now here I was, many years later, listening to my buddy extol the virtue of heroin. He also mentioned that heroin was notorious for helping you sexually -- So, I decided to try it on a small scale -- half of a bag -- and I liked it. I found that I didn't need as much of it to feel good – so I didn't have to steal or cheat people to get it. I felt on top of the world when taking heroin. What I didn't know was that I was beginning to develop a physical dependency, just a week after first trying it my body began to crave it. When I didn't get it, I started to feel sick -- I would feel nauseous, weak, and get tremors. I discovered that heroin brought me the same kind of trouble as crack cocaine – it was just dressed in a different outfit.

Since things were not working out with Michelle, I decided to move back up to Syracuse to stay with my grandmother and try to get away from this new desire. I also moved on to another girl. Though I really liked her (and my grandmother really liked her too), I couldn't help constantly thinking about Michelle.

One day as I was visiting the city, I got into a stare down altercation with a kid from the neighborhood. He was a lot bigger than me, which concerned me, but I could not lose my honor in the neighborhood. In what seemed like a split second, we both stood in the middle of the basketball court while everyone gathered around us. I was already a little drunk and a little nervous about his size, but it was too late -- there was no way to back out gracefully. I looked at him and decided to hit him with the bottle of vodka that I had hidden in a black bag in my hand. In a split second decision, and before he knew what was happening, he was down on the ground. The sheer force and thickness of the vodka bottle broke his cheekbone. The word on the street was that the kid needed major surgery and was furious and looking for me after he left the hospital. He supposedly was planning on bringing some kids from Washington Heights to get me, so I needed to watch my back. And I said to myself I was going to get him before he got me.

A couple of months later I was walking with a few of my friends. I saw him with his friends, but he didn't see me. The code on the street was "Hit em quick and make it count" so I ran up behind him and jumped on him. This time, I happened to have a small beer bottle in my hand, and so I hit him before he could hit me. Within seconds I heard some sirens and we all began running through the avenue in different directions. I, like a magnet, drew the attention of detectives, and they of course caught me. I got arrested because the police officers were told that I tried to rob him, which was not true at all.

Meanwhile, Michelle returned to New York and we started speaking on the phone again. When she heard about my arrest, she came to visit me. After I was released, I went back up to Syracuse, and over time, Michelle and I dropped the pretense and our relationship became intimate.

Our relationship progressed and got out of control quickly because I was dabbling with the "smack" behind her back. When I was in the city, she would lie to her dad about walking her dog so she could see me. Michelle was raised in a strict pentecostal environment, but she was drawn to the "street life" and was attracted by the excitement of being around me; however, she had no idea about my newfound drug attraction to heroin.

I tried unsuccessfully to slow down the heroin use, but started to think about returning to crack again. All the while I continued seeing Michelle, and about a year into our dating relationship, we decided to take a trip to Cancun, Mexico. Michelle thought it would help us to get away and address some of the issues in our relationship --

like my disappearing all the time. Michelle was suspicious that maybe I had begun seeing someone else behind her back. She didn't know that the only one I had been seeing was Lady Heroin. Still, to save our relationship, I agreed to go to Mexico with her. I decided to smuggle some crack-cocaine onto the plane and made the mistake of having a hit of crack on the trip. The next thing I knew, I was in the throes of full-blown paranoia and desperate for more crack during our vacation in Mexico. I went through all the crack cocaine that I had; and what seemed worse was the fact that I could not get any more drugs right then and there. I didn't know anyone in Mexico where I could go to get my next hit. I immediately went into withdrawal – a feeling of anxiety, paranoia, and psychosis. I felt desperate to get my hands on some more drugs fast, so I was frantic to get back to the United States. I knew I could get some crack there. Michelle and I had a huge fight because she had no idea what was going on, but all the while I was trying to get a change in flight so I could fly home. I was literally preparing to leave her behind in Mexico. All she knew was that I was acting crazy and I kept telling her I was sick, and I would leave her behind in Mexico if she didn't go with me back to the States immediately.

Crazed out of my mind, I rode it out for a couple of hours and actually fell asleep. I waited until we could fly back. As soon as we landed in JFK, we took a cab ride to her house. My mind was racing in the cab; I was anxious and my palms were sweaty. I could almost taste the drugs I was deeply craving. The ride seemed like the longest in my life. I dropped her off at her father's house, and as soon as she entered the door, I put the luggage down and headed straight to my friend's apartment without looking back. I was back in the throes of self-destruction.

A New Development

In the midst of this chaos I found out that Michelle was pregnant with my first son, Nicholas. By the end of 1992, Michelle, who was in the third or fourth month of her pregnancy, would always look for me on the streets of Manhattan because I was always disappearing. I was hiding in the crack and heroin den houses around the neighborhood. She would look for me and beg my parents for information. And though my parents were pretty much estranged from me, they would never give Michelle any information whenever she came searching for me. My mother was strung out herself and could offer no help and my dad was on methadone. He didn't want to hear anything about me, nor did he want me in the house because I was stealing again.

Michelle was left alone to deal with her pregnancy and her father, who had warned her that I was bad news. By this time, Michelle—who had never been exposed to a lifestyle of drugs —began to understand that I was bound to this addiction. When she confronted me, I would give her the best excuses I could think of, but all the signs pointed to my addiction. I had been lying to her, pushing her away, and disappearing on her. Much of my hiding was due to the shame I felt and my desire for her not to see me this way. I was walking around like a zombie—extremely thin and disheveled.

Michelle began researching and asking questions about drugs to better come to terms with my situation. She understood by then that I was an addict who came from a family of people who struggled with addiction. It was overwhelming to Michelle. She had no idea how to handle all of it. She was hurt by the way I treated and rejected her, and she was hurt by my family's silence toward her. All the while, the baby's delivery date was getting closer.

Unbelievably, with all the drama and all the tension, Michelle kept trying to understand what was happening to me and my family. She would talk to me for hours, trying to convince me to go to a drug rehab in the city. On several occasions, Michelle would take me to a rehab facility, and while waiting for my turn to sign in, I would change my mind and escape out the bathroom window and leave her there. I did this to her countless times. Looking back, I know it was the grace of God that kept her there. Somehow, Michelle never gave up, as much as she may have wanted to. When asked what kept her by my side, she explained that she wanted to help me, but more so, she wanted to make sure her unborn child had a father in his or her life. Deep down, Michelle knew she loved me and knew that I had the potential to do something great in life.

However, by the time Michelle was about six months pregnant, she was on the verge of leaving and not looking back. I later learned that Michelle had begun to visit Times Square Church, a nondenominational Christian church in the Broadway Theater District, on the corner of 51st Street and Broadway. She would visit with her sister, Elsie, a sibling with whom she had a frosty relationship. Elsie heard about me as well as Michelle's impending pregnancy and started praying for us. She was also a part of a Spanish ensemble within the choir at Times Square Church, so they began praying for me as well. Their prayers seemed to be ignited by Heaven itself; they were committed to interceding for me. They united in faith and prayer that God would do a miracle since He was the only One who could step in and change the situation.

Michelle also began to pray to God, asking Him if He was real -- if He was the God of her father, a faithful and godly man whom she admired. She knew the Christian terms used in her father's church, but the God of the Bible was not yet real to her. She begged God, that if He were real, to step in to help me so that I could be there for her and our son. And though she fervently prayed for me, Michelle was in a place in life where she was broken as well, and she needed God just as much as I did! Not surprisingly, she started to lose her romantic feelings for me. Though she wanted to walk away, she hung in there.

The final straw came when I missed the birth of my child, my firstborn son, Nicholas. Michelle threatened to leave me for good and take our son to live in New Jersey. I begged her to stay. Michelle's brother-in-law had been hearing testimonies of people who had been delivered from drug addiction through a Christian-based drug program called Genesis. The program was located in Newark, New Jersey. Michelle gave me a final ultimatum—either enroll in the drug program or she would leave me for good. I thought to myself who in the world goes to Newark to get their lives together. All I here most of the time is about people trying to leave Newark!

Eventually, Michelle and her brother-in-law convinced me to try it. Michelle turned out to be an angel in disguise. In fact, she would be the instrument used by God to bring me to Himself.

They made arrangements for me to enter the program through the Director, a lovely Christian woman by the name of Theresa. Michelle told me when and where to show up. She had already decided that if I did not show up, we were done.

But that time I inexplicably showed up and followed through with my word. Michelle didn't believe I would, but God made sure I made it to the program. Looking back on it all, I believe God was working mysteriously behind the scenes through all the circumstances and all the people that surrounded me – to set me free.

CHAPTER 7

GOD IF YOU ARE REAL, STOP ME

The first night that I arrived at Genesis seems like a blur. As soon as I arrived, I started feeling the heroine chip that precedes withdrawal symptoms. The chip is when your body begins to feel like a cold sweat, a chill, almost like the beginning of a cold or flu. You become a bit sluggish and aware your body is on empty (craving more drugs). I told them that I would need a hospital for detox. They challenged me to allow them to pray for me and if I still needed detox we could discuss it in the morning. I slept like a baby that night and woke up the next day without the typical withdrawal symptoms. It was all very weird -- I was tired and hungry but the normal pains and shakes that accompany withdrawal from heroin were not there. What in the world happened?

Genesis was a very unique place. It was a small house in a poor section of North Newark. There was no glamour and no fanfare, but they knew all about the power of God to deliver people from their addictions. There were a lot of men looking to be set free from drug addiction. Their approach was simple: We learned about the Word of God, and we learned what it meant to walk with God. We prayed and asked God to come and touch us. I don't recall all of the events that took place the first couple of weeks because there was so much going on with my body and in my mind as I adjusted to being sober again. One particular thing I do remember was going to a street crusade. A gentleman, by the name of Hector Delacruz, whom I heard was a junkie for eighteen years, was being used by God to perform miraculous healings.

One night, during a street rally, he jumped off the stage, telling a woman in a wheelchair that it was her night -- God was going to heal her. He spoke to her in the name of Jesus to get up from the wheelchair; he then laid hands on her, prayed, and helped her to her feet. You could see that this woman was not accustomed to walking. She struggled with her feet and legs, and she trembled as she got up. But the crowd went crazy with praise for God when she began to walk. I could not believe my eyes – I was a little skeptical about what I had just seen, but it was real. This was not something I was used to or had even believed could happen. Seeing God perform a miracle, through a man who had been a junkie for a long time, had a huge impact on me. It caused me to wonder about the power of God. It awoke in me the reality of God, His love and His mercy.

One day at chapel service, Theresa, one of the leaders at Genesis who I considered my spiritual mom, made an altar call for people to give the reins of their lives over to Jesus; to surrender control of their wills, and to ask for forgiveness for the all the wrong they had done. I responded; and as she began to pray for me, I was suddenly caught up in the moment. I felt light and fell backwards and others just laid me down on the floor. I was still conscious and could hear the prayers and worship that was taking place in the chapel. I wanted to get up, but it felt like someone or something was holding me down. Peace swept over me, and I could see the blue skies and clouds in my mind's eye. A sweet presence seemed to fill the room around me. I knew instinctively that God was in the room and was doing something in my life; He was cleansing my heart. Little did I know that this was only the beginning of my faith journey!

There were several moments at Genesis that were key turning points in my life. On one particular occasion, I had a very distinct dream. I was on a fire escape in NYC and I was coming out of a window with stolen gifts and stuffed animals. I was rushing to get away while holding Barney (a stuffed purple dinosaur that was very popular with children), running towards the roof of a building. Suddenly, I could feel someone approaching me and there was no escape. I looked across the building and noticed a big distance between the next rooftop and myself. I also noticed that there was a circle of people praying on another roof, but I did not know how I could get to them. Suddenly, a strong impression came upon me, telling me to let go of the stolen goods. Once I did, the roof that held the praying circle of people began to move towards me. I was able to walk safely toward them. The person pursuing was also gone. I woke up with an understanding that a follower of Jesus Christ must steal no longer.

During another time at Genesis, we started to get involved with a local church in Jersey City. By that time, I had been in the program for several months. As our group visited Spanish churches, we enjoyed the worship, but often found that the churches only played CDs in the background while people sang. It occurred to a group of us that we wanted to sing for God. We were really not that talented, and no one played any instruments, but we had willing hearts. We prayed and longed to sing for the King. One night, after the church service ended, we started to pray and sing to God. We were just a group of young people caught up in the moment of worship. The spirit of God descended on us and began to baptize us with his Holy Spirit, just like it says in chapter two in the book of Acts. I received this baptism for the first time. With tears of joy, I spoke out in worship. I felt "high" but clean at the same time. I also felt joy and peace like no other, which seared into my mind permanently. Immediately after this, our group started singing at different churches, and the anointing of God would come down as we played instrumental CDs in the background while we sang. God continued to do a number of miracles during my time in the Genesis program.

Marriage

During my time at Genesis, Michelle would often visit along with my son Nicholas, and although Michelle had grown up in church and was attending a strong biblical church, she still had not accepted Christ as her Lord and Savior. My spiritual mother, Theresa, would tell me, "You know, Hector, you really can't have an intimate relationship with Michelle because you're not married, even though you have already been intimate. In the eyes of God, you are going to be held accountable to do what's right. You and Michelle have a baby together, and the right thing to do is to get married and give the child a stable home." "Get married? Who wants to do that?" I thought. My life did not include normalcy, and marriage seemed like something that needed stability and normalcy. It was a faraway thought in a faraway land. But somehow this began to work in my mind and all I wanted to do was please God and make it up to Him for all of the times I had messed up. So I thought whatever I could do, to earn some points in the favor column, I should do. I also thought a lot about Nicholas and what was best for him.

Would he have a father around when he needed to ride his bike?

I remember looking at Michelle one day and telling her that, although we were discussing the idea of marriage, we really couldn't go through with it right now because she wasn't a real Christian who was on the same page with me. What a piece of work I was. Of course that really upset her -- she couldn't understand what I was saying considering all that we had been through, especially since she had stood by me during the worst times of my life. It really hurt her. Here I was telling her that she needed to get her life together with God. However, a couple of weeks later, Michelle went to a service, and the Spirit of God swept over her and she began to cry and worship uncontrollably during an altar call. As God continued to cleanse her, she continued to weep. It was then that she officially surrendered her life to the Lord. Although she had grown up in the church all her life, she never knew God personally. In fact, her knowledge of God was based on the fear of God, not the love of God. The last hurdle was cleared for us to get married.

I still wasn't sure if Michelle and I were ready to get married. Theresa suggested that we go to premarital counseling and so I was introduced to a Pastor named Tony and his wife who taught classes at the program. They had a six-month pre-marital counseling thing. But if I was getting married I wasn't waiting six months and I was already struggling with the whole concept of premarital counseling as it was. Once I made up my mind to get married all I was interested in was making it official, otherwise I would change my mind. Looking back, I wish we had taken the advice and obeyed – but we didn't.

We decided that we were ready to take the plunge after all and planned to get married at City Hall in Manhattan. We did not consult anyone on our decision to forego premarital counseling, and the steps we needed to take to prepare for marriage. In fact, we simply figured that God was able to change whatever He needed to change in our lives to make our marriage successful. What a foolish line of reasoning. Yes, God can cover and fix our crooked paths, and He does work all things for good for them who love Him, but some things we just don't need to go through. We had many struggles early on in our marriage. Besides all the baggage each of us brought into the marriage, we were also severely naïve about what it meant to live out a Godly marriage. In spite of us, God has been good and faithful, and has been the rock in our nearly 25 years of marriage.

One More Run in Me

I wish I could say that the Genesis program fixed me for good. The reality is that I slipped one time while I was there, despite the fact that God was working so powerfully. Out of nowhere an evil thought came into my mind -- "I was only free because I was hidden away in this place. This God thing is not real unless you test it on the streets."

It was a lie from the pit of hell. Somehow I felt I needed to see if I could be drug free in New York City; I needed to test this thing, in spite of the protests of others. But I was different now, I thought. I acted different; I had God in my life, and I had a new way of thinking. After all, I had some Scriptures memorized and I had a big fat Bible that I carried around like a weapon. Besides, if God were all-powerful, couldn't He prevent me from doing the things I shouldn't do?

Somehow I stumbled over the fact that God also gives us free will. We are not robots. He gives us His Word, and He gives us stop signs and streetlights, but I'm afraid I ignored all of the warning signs and proceeded to put myself in the middle of temptation. I forgot the scripture that says "Thou shalt not tempt the Lord your God."

One day, I decided I had enough of the program life. I left to return to Manhattan. The day I left, I blatantly (and arrogantly) said to God, "I am leaving here because I'm tired of it and I want to get high. If you are God, You are going to stop me from getting back on drugs." I got on the train in Newark Penn Station, and suddenly my body began to tremble and shake—as if my body was telling me not to go.

When I got to Midtown Manhattan, there were drugs everywhere—as usual.

Nothing had changed in my neighborhood. I knew where to find the drugs and who sold them; however, when I started visiting my old haunts for drugs, nobody seemed to have any, (or was willing to sell me anything). I tried and tried. It seemed as though everyone had all kinds of excuses as to why they couldn't sell, give, or front me any drugs. I looked for what seemed like an eternity. Finally, out of desperation, I went to my mom's house and convinced her to get me a bag of heroin from my dad's stash. I told her it was for someone else because she knew I was in the program.

She unwillingly relented and gave me a bag and I sniffed it in the hallway of the West 50th Street building where we lived. I sat down and waited for the effects to kick in. I kept waiting for the high, but soon realized that it had no effect—the bag did nothing. "Are you kidding me?" I thought to myself. "I went through all of this trouble for nothing? My Dad is selling some garbage. They must have given me something that is no good." At no point did I stop to consider that perhaps God was interceding and stopping me in my tracks.

Unfortunately for me, I wasn't able to recognize or acknowledge God's efforts to stop me. The Lord had given me several ways to escape temptation, but I didn't take them. Instead, I ran straight toward sin with my arms wide open. That first night, I ended up staying out on the streets to make sure I got high, and I had the worst time doing it. The Bible says that when we go back to our old ways, the demonic spirit comes back to find the house empty and swept clean, so it comes back with seven other spirits and makes matters worse. That was exactly how it felt—everything was worse. The depth of my despair was worse; and the drug usage became worse as well.

Once again, I turned to my drug selling abilities to maintain my addiction. I also went back to stealing from everybody, including my parents, when I ran out of drugs or money. I developed a keen business mind; being able to purchase a ten-dollar piece of crack cocaine, flip it for thirty dollars, only to race back uptown on the train to purchase more. I would jump the turnstile so I would have exactly what I needed to purchase the drugs. Whenever I played my cards right, I would have my supply and enough to sell to keep the cycle rolling. My mom always allowed me to enter their home, and she never turned me away, even though we both knew what we were doing was wrong. It got to the point where I was buying cocaine and sharing it with my mom. It was weird, but we had come to a place where we had accepted that we were both drug addicts.

That, as they say, was the price of doing business.

My time on the streets was dark and grimy. I was up for days on end; hungry, thirsty, and losing weight. I was damaging my health and my mind.

Spiritually, I was lost and broken, but even in the midst of my chaos, God did not give up on me or turn his back on me. God does not know how to fail; he always finishes what He starts. I believe God was using this situation to wake me up and to permanently change me. He was destroying the desire for this thing in my life. He was not only taking me out of the streets but also removing the streets from my heart. He allowed me to compare the ways of death and bondage with the ways of God and freedom.

The nights were cold and long on the streets – I was always scheming and looking for my next opportunity. Some nights it was a ghost town in Hell's Kitchen -- only zombies were out; like the walking dead searching endlessly for fulfillment that could not be found on the streets.

We scratched and clawed desperately to find what we were looking for. We all chased the feeling of the first hit of crack and the first bag of heroine; but in reality we were all just chasing the wind.

CHAPTER 8

⌘

A WIFE WHO PRAYS

Michelle was back to looking for me but not like before. I kept avoiding her as I struggled with a greater sense of failure -- a feeling that maybe not even God could fix me. There seemed to be no way out. But my God is a way-maker. He specializes in making a way out of no way . . .

Michelle continued to pray and attend Times Square Church in Midtown Manhattan. Desiring guidance, Michelle started counseling with some of the pastors at church. She wanted to know what her position and role should be as my wife; and whether or not it was right for her to go forward with a divorce. My new wife was depleted from all that she had been through with me and she was also concerned how my addiction would impact our son.

In the meantime prayer surrounded me. The Genesis Program members, including Theresa, were praying for me — that God would complete what He had started and not allow the devil or my addiction to destroy me. The weapon of prayer is powerful! The God who hears our cry is ALL-powerful! When the people of God start praying fervently, things begin to happen [even when nothing appears to be happening outwardly]. *The kingdom of darkness suffers violence when Gods people pray...* In other words, as believers, the weapons of our warfare are spiritual and mighty and able to pull down strongholds. There was no doubt that my stronghold was drug addiction.

But, when we pray, we invite God and all of heaven to act and move on our behalf. When God is for us who can stand against us? No one can win a fight against God!

As people continued to pray for me, I knew outwardly that I was back in the desert. I understood that my journey was just like the one the Jews experienced in the Book of Exodus. I had been rescued from a severe form of slavery and was trying to find my way back into it. I was fighting against my freedom. I wanted to be back in the grips of "Pharaoh." I had been delivered from Egypt but I kept looking back toward it and desiring to be back with my cruel taskmaster. Can you relate to this? Have you ever felt like you knew something was wrong and yet it seemed you had no power to turn away from it? Maybe it's an abusive relationship yet you keep coming back for more. Or you have an addiction, and try as you may; it just seems to have you in its grips.

My wife was my own personal intercessor, battling before God that I would be set free for good through prayer and faith. But I was right back in the clutches of Satan, staying up days at a time, without much sleep. The crack cocaine kept me going. I was losing so much weight: the drug was my only food.

Somewhere along the journey, I became depressed and plummeted to a place where I was physically and mentally exhausted. I wanted out, but didn't know how to get out of this desert wasteland that was my life. I knew I was destroying my family and myself. In my heart, I had the knowledge that Jesus was real, but that knowledge of Him was not enough to get me off the streets. I didn't know how to humble myself and cry out to God. I didn't know how to surrender to Him, and to make matters worse. I was under the deception that God would no longer take me back. I felt (and too often believed) that I was forever lost; forever dirty; and forever a criminal and a junkie. But it was a lie, a lie from the enemy himself to keep me in bondage.

But, God was there and I knew it each time His grace and mercy came to my rescue.

There were times when I was out on the streets and I would get an urgent sense that I needed to leave. Whenever I obeyed that voice and left, the police would come right after and arrest people. Each time, I would escape by the skin of my teeth.

On more than one occasion, I'd find myself using in a base house, only to abruptly sober up. My high would just disappear. Without being able to stop myself, I would begin to talk about Jesus. I could feel His presence all around me. I'd start thinking about eternity without God, and get a very real sense of its reality. Each time the high evaporated, I would just sit there, stone, cold sober, talking to everybody about what I had learned about Jesus! I'd warn everyone in that crack house about the fact that Jesus could come back at any moment. I told them that if He did, I, along with everyone in that base house, would be lost. I kept speaking about our sinful state and living a life of wickedness.

And when people heard me saying such things, they would say things like, "This guy is crazy, and he's hallucinating." Or they would say, "You are killing my high, man." I couldn't believe it. Even when I had the pipe in my mouth, and was using my hands to fill it with crack-cocaine, God was on my mind. Can you imagine the controversy in my soul? I had crack on my hand, smoke in my lungs, crack pipe in my mouth, and Jesus on my mind. Lord help me!

I couldn't block Him out no matter how much I tried. It was as if God was coming through the walls to get me. He wanted to set me free from my prison cell and my chains. The night I was arrested the officer had warned me previously to get out of the building because he would be back to check in, but I would not listen. I believe it was actually God's will that I be arrested that day. I was rescued from the wreckage that was my life!

I did not know it at the time but this was the last time I would be arrested. God was saying to my addiction, "This far and no farther." I saw it as being rescued from my misery. As I sat in the police car, all I could do was let out a huge sigh. I had reached a point where I was completely tired of my lifestyle. When I got to Central Booking that night I was so exhausted that I fell asleep on the cold dirty floor. In fact, I was so tired that I don't even remember going through the process of incarceration. When I woke up, I was sent to stand in front of the judge, and with a record like mine, it was expected that I would be sent back to Riker's Island – C95.

Michelle was exhausted too. She was drained from all of the drama, arrests, and disappearances. She told me she no longer wanted anything to do with me. She had decided to divorce me and wanted full custody of our son, Nicholas. How could I blame her? One day I went to church service in jail and while everyone was singing I started to sense the presence of God and weep; but I still wasn't in a position where I felt like God could forgive me. I felt like I had messed up a great opportunity He had given me, and that there was no forgiveness left for my disobedience. I didn't know the love of God and that His mercy would pursue me. And I didn't know just how long-suffering God is -- that he had come to set the captives free.

Yet the Lord and his love broke through my distress and said, "You are mine."

The Dream that Changed Everything

In January of 1995, I had a dream.

In this dream, I was on a piece of fence that was floating in midair. People were walking on the streets below me, including three men walking with wolves on leashes. The wolves had sheep's clothing on. Suddenly they released the wolves and the wolves were trying to attack me, as I remained perched on the fence. I knew that if I fell the wolves would tear me to pieces.

Out of nowhere I heard a distant call for breakfast. The call for chow inside C-95 became louder and louder and I woke up terrified. When I went to breakfast that morning I tried to shake off the dream. "It was just a nightmare and nothing more," I told myself. "There was really nothing significant about it."

But, when I went back to sleep that morning, the dream picked up right where it left off. *I was back on the fence and floating in the air. The wolves were released to attack me. All of a sudden, I remembered I could call on the name of Jesus in the midst of trouble and began to cry out, "Jesus, Jesus help me, they're trying to kill me!" All of a sudden the pictures in the dream changed -- I was back in my mother's house and inside my bedroom, standing behind a small wooden pulpit with an open Bible. There were people waiting for me to speak.*

I woke up and instinctively knew that this dream was different. Strangely, it seemed God was trying to speak to me. I got on my knees and prayed as I struggled to try to decipher what it all meant and remember all the details. I sensed that it had to do with my battle for freedom from bondage and I remember sensing that this was all related to my present situation.

I started to sense God's *answer*. I didn't hear an audible voice, but I could almost *feel* what God was saying. He was telling me that I was on the fence; I was between two opinions, high above all that the world had to offer, but I had allowed the wolves to drag me back down to the streets. I was going to go back on the fence for a season and I was being warned not to allow the wolves—the things of this world—to drag me back down.

I kept praying, asking God for a clue as to the Bible verse opened in my dream. Deep inside, I knew that there was significance to that verse. Out of nowhere, I heard a still small voice say, "Galatians five."

I had never read Galatians 5 before that day. In the NIV version it says, *"It is for freedom that Christ has set you free. Stand firm then and do not let yourself be burdened again by a yoke of slavery.* Another part says, *"You were running a good race, who cut in on you and kept you from obeying the truth. That kind of persuasion does not come from the One who has called you."* And then it says, *"You, my brothers, are called to be free, but do not use that freedom to indulge the sinful nature."*

I knew this was God speaking -- confirming what I was going to go through but also where I was going to end up. God had a plan for me. Oh what a joy and sudden jolt to know that God was still willing to speak to me.

Before I knew it, I repented and asked God to cleanse me; to renew the work he had started in my heart and life. I believe that was the beginning of the end with the drugs that had been in my life. I did not want to be the same person. I cried out to God, "If I'm going to leave here still addicted to drugs, going back to cause pain, leave me here in the prison."

But God had another plan for me. Instead of praying for God to leave me in prison, He led me to pray, "God, just change my life." If I wanted freedom, I must have God change my desires.

I called my wife and told her God spoke to me the night before. I shared how God told me that He was going to put us together again and that I would be free.

Michelle said, "Well, He never spoke to me about it!" In other words, "Back up son." Being a Christian is more than having the right church language and Bible verses on your lips and memorized; it's about following and trusting a God who transforms. And it's all about fruit -- a lifestyle to back up your words. It was clear that she didn't want to hear it. And again, how could I blame her?

Michelle then said, "Hector, you haven't changed. You only have the language of a Christian, but not the walk to back it up." We ended our discussion, and though

Michelle was not very receptive, I was renewed with a sense that God had given me a second chance. And this time – this time I didn't want to ruin my chance. I mean my life had more drama than a ten-year soap opera. This time I would not let Him go until He blessed me.

After several days had passed, Michelle said she had this overwhelming feeling that was telling her to get some money from her father to bail me out. Her father was a Pentecostal, born-again Christian, who didn't want anything to do with me. Who could blame him after everything I had put his daughter through? Yet, by the grace of God, her father eventually gave her the money to bail me out.

The night prior to my being bailed out from Riker's Island, my mind began to wander. Like always, I started thinking about going back home -- back to the old neighborhood, and back to my old friends. My mind became filled with images and feelings about drugs. Once again, it was almost as if I had forgotten that I had given my heart and vowed to the Lord. However, as my mind kept wandering, I suddenly sensed God speaking into my consciousness. He said, "Look at what is in your heart and what you're thinking of."

I sat in the cell, frozen as these thoughts washed over me. I felt ashamed, and could barely face it. All I could do was sit there, repenting. "Forgive me, God," I kept saying over and over. "Please, forgive me." I wanted to be free. It was cemented in my heart and spirit that if He would get me out, I would go straight to church and give Him full reign over my life.

CHAPTER 9

DAMNED TO DESTINED

After being released on bail, my wife and I were on the train going back to Midtown Manhattan. Michelle turned to me and said, "What's wrong? You don't seem happy."

I looked her in the eyes and said, "I can't stay with you and Nicholas yet. I have a long journey of recovery ahead, and I have to start out by going to the Timothy House."

Timothy House was a Christian drug program run by Times Square Church. Though Michelle was confused by my decision, I felt strongly that this was the road I needed to take so that God could finally fix me and I could live my life for Jesus. Our marriage, and my son, needed a drug free dad – and the Timothy House was the step I needed to take to build a solid foundation. I needed to pass the exam that I failed at Genesis. I signed myself into the Timothy House where I stayed for a couple of months.

Pastor William Carroll and John Foster were in charge of the program. I began turning my life over to the care of God as I understood Him at that time -- allowing Him to take everything—everything that I was, had gone through, and had done. I admitted to God that I was powerless and that my life was unmanageable. I wanted a fresh start. While in the program, I also started to develop a relationship with Pastor Richie Weiss, who was in charge of the Prison Ministry at Times Square Church. As I waited for my court case, we started to pray and fast for God's favor—specifically, for Him to dismiss the case. During that time, I had a desire to go to the Mt Zion School of Ministry to become someone God could use.

God, however, had another plan for me.

A couple of months into the Timothy House program, my court date came due. Pastor Richie came with me to be a visible support and possibly sway the judge and the District Attorney. Unfortunately, the judge had other ideas. The judge barked and motioned to my attorney that my record was extensive and advised him that I should consider the plea bargain that the DA had offered me. If I did not take the plea bargain, the judge indicated he was going to give me the maximum sentence under the law if I went to trial and lost. A minimum sentence, for a three-time felon, can start at twenty-five-years-to-life. There wasn't much to think about. I knew I had to take that plea bargain because I was guilty, but also because there were no other options. The pressure was on. My head was spinning. I couldn't understand how – if I had all of Heaven on my side – people praying, a pastor coming with me to court – how could I lose my case? The plea deal was for me to take 3 to 6 years otherwise I would stand trial. I decided to take the deal, and the judge gave me a date to return to court to be sentenced. I only had about six weeks of freedom left.

Needless to say, even though I was guilty, and even though I deserved far worse, I was disappointed about having to return to prison for no less than three years. I just didn't understand how this could be part of God's will for my life. After all, isn't going to Bible school better than going to jail? There is no rehab going back to jail.

As I was exiting Manhattan Criminal Court, the phrase, "Can you still praise me now?" was impressed upon my heart and over-powered my thoughts. I said, "God, I praise you. I love you. I'm going to serve you no matter what comes my way."

I went back to the Timothy House and thanked Pastor Richie for coming to court. I was distraught about having to go back to prison, but everything seemed different and brighter in my life now. There were people at the Timothy House who wondered why I chose to remain in the program instead of being with my wife and child. But, I knew that God had a purpose for my being there.

He finally had full control of my life, and I truly sensed that He didn't want me to be home – not yet.

A week before my prison sentence start date, I spent a week with my wife and son. The morning of surrendering myself to serve my prison sentence, my mind was a storm of thoughts and my heart was a flood of feelings. I realized that if I had listened to God the first time He cleaned me up, I could have been studying the Bible at the Mt. Zion School of Ministry. I could have been already pursuing the goals God was starting to put in my heart, and I could have been with my wife and son. Instead I was going to prison and leaving Michelle to provide and take care of our family alone. I wrestled with the burdens I had put on my wife and I asked God who would take care of my family while I was gone.

I had to check into prison at 1pm. Right before I was due to leave the house, Michelle called me and was ecstatic. "Honey, I just got called into my boss's office. He just offered me a raise," she exclaimed. Michelle had only been on the job about four months and hadn't even passed the probation period. Regardless, the raise was given and that was a sign to me from God that this was His plan and purpose—and that I was to go and serve my sentence in peace.

God's Plan at Work – In Prison

I turned myself in, and they let me keep my Bible. This time I was in C74. I have to admit, I found myself angry that I was in prison and would ask the Lord, "God, why am I here again? I could have gone to Mt Zion or become a missionary." I kept wondering why God did not spare me the consequences of my actions, especially since I was finally serious about changing my life.

That first night, a young man who was in the cell next to me came in and said, "You know what you have been telling me today about this Jesus? Well, I've thought about it and I want to ask Jesus to come into my life. I really do want Him to change me. Is it alright for me to do it right here and now inside this cell?" I smiled at him, and right then and there, we prayed for salvation and forgiveness.

The light bulb came on in my head. I instinctively knew at that moment that God wanted me to take His message of forgiveness, salvation, and hope inside the prison walls while preparing me for something else. Can you believe it? There was a purpose for me to be in prison. Not just the fact of "doing my time," but a godly purpose – a calling directly from the Lord.

The next day I got up, excited about God's plan for me. I started giving out Bible tracts in the prison and people would look at me and say, "Man, what's wrong with you? This isn't 42nd Street." However, I didn't care about what they said because I was on patrol -- on duty for Jesus.

I spent my time in prison seeking the Lord. I would spend hours studying the Word of God. I would go to sleep reading the Bible and wake up reading the Bible. It was my Bible seminary time.

God began to do wonderful things in my life. He began to teach me the plan of salvation and teach me that salvation was not of works—good behavior—but of faith in Him through Jesus Christ. I also learned that "good works" may come as a result of my love for Him, and could be a demonstration of my faith in Him, but could never save me. It was wonderful. I felt so good about what God *was doing* in my life. I finally started to understand what He had *already done* in my life through the power of Jesus Christ.

As is customary in the penal system, I kept getting transferred to different jails, so much so that I would lose track of where I was and where I had been. I went to one prison where there was a brother named Mike, and he would often debate with guys in another cell. They would talk about the fact that some people didn't believe in Jesus; some people believed in Muhammad; and yet others believed in science instead of a divine being. There was even a sect of black men who called themselves, "Five-Per Centers," and they believed that the black man was God and would refer to themselves as "god."

One day Mike was having a debate with this group about whether or not God was real. Mike finally came into my cell and asked me to join their debate in the other cell. There was a guy there who said he believed we evolved from monkeys. I sensed a question rise up in my spirit and so I asked the question, "If we came from Monkeys how is it that the monkeys aren't changing over anymore? When did that stop? Why don't the monkeys change in the zoos?" He didn't have a response. Neither did anyone else. The next statement in the debate was about not believing in anything we couldn't see and that we were foolish because no one had ever seen God. I proceeded to make a statement about how we all believe in the air yet we don't see it. Just like our lives depend on the air to breath and live likewise we also depend on God for life.

I proceeded to share about the love of Jesus with these inmates and how God would change their lives; right down to the very things they were still involved in. After the debate, Mike and I went back to my cell. There was a young Spanish guy, who had been sitting quietly during the debate. He shared that his mother had been praying for him. This young man had been serving the Lord at one time, but had turned away to get involved with the street lifestyle. Unfortunately, prison was the consequence.

After the debate, the young man came into my cell and said, my mom has been praying for me and believes in God. "Can I accept Jesus right now and ask him to change me? Can He still forgive me -- can he change my life as you say?"

I simply said, "Absolutely."

"What do I have to do to be saved?" The kid asked.

I said, "Just lift up your arms right now, surrender your life, and cry out to Jesus."

I began to pray for him and Mike started to pray for him. All of a sudden Mike begins to cry out in worship and drops to his knees speaking in another tongue, right there in the cell. Then the other inmate went down on the ground in the cell. The presence of God swept over him. There were other inmates walking by watching, and I was in the middle of both of these men—one was speaking in another tongue, while the other was on the ground. The power of God fell in the cell!

The news spread through the prison system. Many people were walking around saying, "Don't let those guys pray for you." They didn't understand that we had nothing to do with it—it was all the power of the Holy Spirit.

One day I was at the commissary store waiting for my food. There was this big African-American brother who started telling me about his problems. He told me that he had pain in his body. I asked him if I could pray for him and he said, "No, no, no I don't want you to pray for me—I heard about you guys, and I don't want weird stuff happening to me."

He Watches Over Me

I was transferred to a prison in upstate New York and started working in the mess hall. One day a guy came through and started to curse at me because he wanted more food, and I wasn't allowed to give any more. He threatened me and said that if he saw me in the yard, he was going to do something to me.

Of course, the day came when I was in the yard, and sure enough he walked toward me with a couple of other men and began to threaten me.

At the same time, there were two guys standing in the yard watching the whole confrontation. In fact, these two guys slept in my dormitory area, and I had been speaking to them about Jesus and his power to change a life. They were the leaders of two dominant Spanish gangs in the prison—one was in the Latin Kings the other was in the Nieta Gang. They went over and told the guy that if he ever approached me in that fashion again, he wouldn't be leaving the prison on his own. The protection of the Lord was all around me. God showed me how He was powerful enough to use two gang members to do His work if He wanted to. In fact, these two guys were the very two men that I was sharing the love of Jesus within the dorms.

From that prison, I was shipped to Marcy Correctional Facility where I was given the opportunity to do less time in prison if I participated in a drug treatment program run by Phoenix House. They said if I passed through a rigorous course of treatment, I would be free from jail.

I joined the Phoenix House program. We were isolated from the rest of the prison population, living and breathing a Twelve-Step Program. Part of the therapy included group confrontations where we yelled and screamed at each other for exhibiting behaviors that led us to use drugs. Once again the Lord granted me favor with the authorities and I became one of the leaders in this program.

Early in 1996, as I was still going through the program, my wife received a call about an apartment. She turned the apartment down because I wasn't going to be coming home any time soon. She received another call in the middle of the year, which she also turned down. Finally, in the fall of 1996, when I was on the brink of being released from the program, she received a third call. She accepted the apartment because I was about to come home. The Lord prepared my home before I even got there. He cares about even the smallest details of our lives!

I was released at the end of 1996. Following a short stay at a halfway house in the Bronx, I was finally living again with my wife, Michelle, on West 54th Street and 10th Avenue. We were finally living together as a family with our son, Nicholas. This was a miracle in and of itself. Because I was given favor from God, I was given what was called "7-0 Status," meaning seven days out in the community and zero days in the work release jail. Usually when an inmate is given a work release, they are sent to a facility in Washington Heights, and given a status such as "four days out, three days in," or something similar. This allowed the ex-convict to be slowly integrated into the community, while being monitored, until they reached the "7-0 Status." God allowed me to have 7-0 status immediately upon my release, which was extremely rare in those days.

CHAPTER 10

FREE AT LAST

Pastor Richie who continued to invest in my life, offered me a job cleaning the streets of Times Square . . . A job was the other variable needed for me to get my 7-0 status for release.

As I understood at the time, Times Square Church had an arrangement with The Times Square Business Improvement District, also known as the Times Square BID, and hired me at $5.00 per hour to clean the streets. While it may not have seemed like much of a job, it was a huge first step for me, as I began to re-acclimate myself to society and live a normal life. It was also a chance to work – a genuine opportunity since most ex-convicts rarely get a fair shot at being employed. Sad to say, though we talk a lot about second chances in our culture, most ex-cons never really get a fair chance. We can't get past the question on the application; "Have you ever been convicted of a crime," which is the death nail for most ex-offenders who want to try to make things right.

I looked at my job as a miracle from God, and I took it very seriously. Not long after I started the cleaning job, my wife bumped into a gentleman with whom she used to work. He asked her if she needed a job, and she said no but told him that her husband could use an opportunity. A few days later we sent him my resume, which he passed on to someone else in his company. Time passed, but one day I was called for an interview.

Group Health Incorporated --The Beginning of Stability

I couldn't remember the last time I had actually interviewed for a job. Though the job was for an entry-level clerical position, I prepared as if it were an executive position. When I stepped into the office to be interviewed, a man and a woman were waiting for my arrival. Early on in the interview, it was evident that the man was not fond of me and was not planning to give me the job. He looked at my resume and frowned, "Mr. Vega, there are a lot of gaps in your resume." I thought to myself, what does he mean gaps, I made sure I filled up the entire page. Then I realized he was alluding to the missing years on my resume.

I didn't want to lie, but I couldn't conceive of telling him the truth and then him giving me the job. Seriously, how many ex-offenders go through this and are successful?

I sat there, constructing a detailed explanation in my mind about how I had done odd jobs "under the table" during those years that were not listed on my resume. But suddenly, I could feel that lying was wrong and, if I had decided to follow God, then He was in the interview and I needed to trust Him with the outcome. Taking a deep breath, I proceeded to tell them about my substance abuse problem and my time in correction.

The man nodded as if to say, "I knew it. I found you out." However, the woman looked at me kindly and threw me a bone when she asked me, "Well, did you do anything while you were there?"

I answered, "Well, of course. I went through the Twelve-Step programs, as well as the Phoenix House Halfway House. I also had the opportunity to be a Coordinator for the program..."

Colleen, the woman interviewing me, continued to ask me a series of questions that allowed me to discuss my time while incarcerated, in a positive way. It was obvious that God was at work giving me favor. Through Colleen's questions I was given the opportunity to describe the many positive ways that I excelled in the prison programs, and how I was working on getting my life back on track. This became my lifeline in the interview and turned the tide from being awkward to upbeat.

Though I didn't get that particular job, a few weeks later Colleen called and asked me if I still wanted to work for GHI. There was another job opportunity available that paid more and all I needed to do was come in and take a test. I saw God move with favor on my behalf and favor became the theme of my life. I was blessed and highly favored. Telling the truth gave me the opportunity to see that I didn't have to lie to get ahead. I knew I could trust God with my career.

I went into the GHI office the very next day and took the exam. After seeing the results, Colleen offered me the position. I asked her if I could get back to her because I needed to pray about it. She looked bewildered, and said, "Pray?" I said, "Yes, trust me, I have made a lot of mistakes and I want God to be a part of every detail of my life." She gave me a couple of days to respond.

At the same time I was involved with Times Square Church and was being asked about possibly working in the church annex as part of security. I really wanted to work for the church, so I asked my mentor, Pastor Richie, what I should do. He said, "What's the matter with you? You have a family. You have benefits with the job position at GHI, and the church can't pay you what they can pay you. Besides, you will learn new skills that will help you go farther with GHI. I think you need to take this job right away."

I called Colleen and told her I would accept the position but I still had a concern. "You see, there is this man that follows me and shows up without notice," I said. She instinctively understood that I was talking about my Parole officer. Colleen said, "Don't worry Hector, I will give you my phone number and whenever he shows up he can call me and I will have you released to meet him outside. This way no one knows your business."

God was at work fighting my battles.

I went through a twelve-week job-training program and passed with flying colors. I then had to pass the transitional period—another twelve weeks— as well as a probationary period while "on the floor." After about only four months, the department that I worked for within GHI (HIP hospital customer service), lost their contract and the department was going to be dissolved. I was a temporary employee, so I didn't have the same rights as the regular union employees; I had no rights to be placed in another department within the company.

But, I was exactly where God wanted me -- in a place where all I could do was trust Him to work on my behalf. My Supervisor, Theresa, asked me what I was going to do now that we had lost the contract and that I was not part of the union. I told her that I didn't know, but that I would like to stay with the company. She called Human Resources for me and encouraged them to find a place for me because she felt I was a good employee. Once again, God showed me His grace and favor. Theresa became my internal advocate. Thanks to her perseverance, Human Resources found another position for me in the Data Matching Department. An interview was scheduled, but, before I attended, Theresa informed me that it was a long shot because the position in Data Matching was all but spoken for by someone who was well connected. Still, they gave me the opportunity to meet with the supervisor and an HR representative in that department.

The interview went very well and the supervisor assured me that I would hear something very soon and that they would reconsider their position on the other applicant. I was called by the HR representative, a second time, and she informed me that the department supervisor was impressed and they offered me the position as a Data Match Clerk—even though the position was already spoken for. Again, God had shown up as my lawyer and my advocate. My time in data match was awesome. My supervisor embraced me as if I had been part of her team for a long time. She found out that my wife was expecting a second child and she encouraged the department to help us with gifts and money. Praise God for His favor. Some months passed and I successfully completed my probationary period and became a full-time employee with all the union benefits.

All through my time at GHI, God gave me a supernatural favor with the people I worked for. They had a significant amount of loyalty and love in their heart for me—beyond anything I did with regard to my work.

Surrounded by God's Grace and Gracious People
The gracious people that the Lord has brought into my life have amazed me; even my parole officer, showed tremendous grace in his interactions with me. For the first

time ever, I was being monitored by a stand-up guy. He didn't hassle me like the previous parole officers had done. He saw that I was trying to do the right thing and keep my nose clean.

One time, my parole officer said to me, "Hector, I can sense you're doing the right thing and can see this God thing is really working for you." He even went so far as to buy my wife and me a gift for our second child. Can you believe it? My parole officer got a gift for my baby. They rarely give their parolees any room to breathe, let alone buy their parolees anything. This PO however, was a kind man. I sensed that he was a Christian. He did do his job though— monitoring me, checking on me at work, and verifying what I was doing with my time. Not once did he hassle me, demean me, or stalk me like the previous POs did.

To this day, I am amazed at how much God maneuvered in my life through people like my Parole Officer, Theresa, and so many others. God certainly used people from the church to assist me, but it was even more amazing to witness how He used people outside of the church community; to help me transition out of prison and into the work force so I could become a productive member of society. And God wasn't done with His work in me. He continued to do miraculous things.

After working for a year as a Data Match Clerk, I realized that I wanted to start doing other things and gain other skills. I applied for a position in the Customer Service

Department, passed the test, and got the job. Amazingly, not only did I get the position, which came with a paid training program, I was also able to help my wife, Michelle, get into the same paid training program. Michelle and I both finished the classes, obtained Customer Service positions, and received significant salary increases.

God's favor continued as I grew in the GHI family. Every department I transitioned into, in every new position, God continued to grant me favor with the heads of those departments. I was given opportunities to do more than my position required which allowed me to acquire new skills and experience, all of which helped advance my career. I continued to move forward at GHI, even with my lack of education and work history. You could say that God filled in the blanks on my behalf. And all the while he was preparing me for a bigger place; a place of greater responsibility.

Interestingly enough, not everyone was happy with my work performance. In fact, the union had an issue with my hard work ethic. Union leads often approached me and warned me that I was making other employees look bad for going above the call of duty. They went so far as directing me not to continue doing things with this standard.

In spite of their threatening tone, I decided to continue doing what God led me to do. I knew that, as a Christian, I was to do my job to the very best of my ability – to give it my all. After all, it was God making the provisions for me and not the union. I did my job as if God was my boss!

Around that time, I got myself involved with the company's baseball team. I always had a love for baseball and was good at it. Being on the company's baseball team afforded me the opportunity to meet various people in the company, including supervisors and department heads I wouldn't normally encounter in the course of my work. I was able to make wonderful contacts, which included the CEO's son. I was also able to network and hear the latest information about what was going on, above me, in the company.

A short while after joining the baseball team, I learned about an Account Services Representative position that sounded intriguing. The job included going out into the community to meet with individual groups that were insured by GHI. The position was flexible in that I would work out in the field some days and in the office on other days.

I got to know a man named Don Harper who played on the baseball team. I discovered that Don was the Director of this division, however I chose not to discuss the position with him. Instead I decided I would simply apply for one of the Account Service Representative positions and allow God to provide me with the job if it was His will. By then, I had realized that God had granted me so many blessings and miracles at this company, that He could do anything! The Word of God says *"the eyes of the Lord run to and fro throughout the whole earth, to show Himself strong on behalf of those whose heart is loyal to Him."*

I applied for the position and aced the mandatory exam. I was required to put together a presentation for other company employees -- a mixture of Human Resources, department supervisors, and other account services representatives. After completing all phases of the interview, I was offered the position.

Unfortunately, right after that, the top Union Representative stepped in to cry "foul." She had heard that I played baseball with Don Harper, the Director of that division, and demanded to see my test scores to determine if there had been any favoritism in the hiring process. I discovered that the leader of the union had wanted someone else to get this position even though I had earned the job fair and square. The union representative worked something out with the Training Department Manager in order to review my test scores. Once she did, she disqualified one of the answers. As a result, my test score was lowered a percentage or two, which meant that someone else scored higher and could be offered the job over me. I ended up losing the position. I was incredulous.

Upset over the union leaders' persistence to sabotage my victory, I resolved that I would no longer allow myself to be subject to the union. In fact, I wanted my union dues money back. It seemed like yet another trial for me to go through, but before I could become bitter, God answered my prayer. Almost immediately, a non-union management position became available in the training department. It was a Quality Analyst position. As it turned out, that position was responsible for monitoring the work of Account Service Representatives, the very position that the union's chief swindled me out of. The Quality Analyst was a senior position with a higher salary. Again, I participated in the interview and met with the training department head.

During the application process, I learned that I would no longer be eligible for the union's protection – which included a structured pay raise schedule and additional benefits. If I stayed in the union, I would pretty much be guaranteed a job for life. But, I knew that if I stepped out in faith, and allowed God to take me to unchartered territory it could take my career to a different level.

I decided to do just that. I trusted God and continued with the application process.

I met with the Director of the Training Department and he was very encouraging. He saw that I was motivated and felt that I had potential to transition into management. That same day, I had to meet with the Manager of Human Resources.

She started the interview with small talk but then went right to the point. She said, "Look Hector, the Director wants to offer you this position, but first I have one question. As I look at your resume, before GHI, you have a lot of missing time. I want to know what happened." I looked her straight in the eyes and said, "Ms. Taylor,

I had some substance abuse problems and my life had become a mess." She stopped me from saying anything else and said, "I just wanted to see if you would tell the truth. You got the job."

I moved into my new management position and found out I would also be supervising the individual who was given my union position of Account Service Representative. My professional life was, in some ways, beginning to resemble the life of Joseph.

In the midst of my career journey, I began to realize just how much God was in control. I was thankful that God specifically led me to a company where the questions, regarding the applicant's history, were not a prominent part of the application process. I had been given many opportunities within this family-run business and there was no doubt in my mind that God had orchestrated every single part of it.

A New Identity

God's mercy became even more magnified after I was given the Quality Analyst position. A short time after beginning my position, I became a part of the Human Resources division. One day, I attended a seminar in which they utilized a role-play activity. The gentleman who was leading it used words to describe someone or someplace, and we had to guess what he was describing.

He said, "I'm skinny, fat, short, tall, black, white, blue eyes, brown eyes—who am I?"

We went around the room but nobody was able to figure it out. I shouted out, "It sounds like you are describing a human being" He said, "Close, but no cigar. I'm describing an ex-convict."

One woman in the room said, "Wow, I never looked at it that way. It could be anyone. We have a picture in our head that it's this type of person, but an ex-con can be anyone -- it can be anyone we interview for a job."

Ironically, there I was, sitting right in the midst of these people. I was an ex-con and nobody seemed to know. I looked at the lady next to me and said, "Hey you want to hear a secret? I'm really an ex-con." She said, "Yeah, right." Then she said, "If you are an ex-con, I am an ex-nun."

Right then and there, I sensed God was letting me in on a divine revelation. I felt Him say to me in my heart, *"Look how far I have brought you. You WERE an ex-con, but not anymore. Look at the people around you. They don't even believe you were once a convict. I have changed you, Hector – I have transformed you. You are a new creation – you are now MY son!"* He who the Son sets free is free indeed!

God took me from life on the streets – a drug addict; a thief; an ex-convict – and placed me in the middle of mainstream society; working in a management-level position, restored with a sound mind and with a spirit of love and power. People did not [and could not] see me as I used to be—even when I attempted to share it with them. They could only see what God had done. They only saw me in my present state and could not fathom my past.

I took on that position with a vengeance, determined to do my best to honor God and all He had done to bring me to where I needed to be. After working in the training department as a Quality Analyst for a period of time, God again, gave me favor and I was promoted to be a Corporate Trainer. It was a significant accomplishment because most of the trainers, if not all, were people who had experience in the GHI Claims Department. I was working alongside them, yet I had nothing other than my background in the customer service department.

I have been working at GHI since 1997 and have seen the miraculous favor of God time and time again. He is still using me in the workplace, even as he develops me and allows me to provide for my family; however, I discovered that my work at GHI was not all that God had planned for me.

CHAPTER 11

⌁

RISING OUT OF THE ASHES

I joined the Raven Ministry at (Times Square Church), which is a street evangelism team that goes into the community to share the Gospel with the homeless and the broken. Every Wednesday, my wife and I joined the foot soldiers who visited homeless people in cardboard boxes and, on Saturdays, I visited the single room occupancy hotels on the west side of 22nd and 23rd street. We brought food and the love of God to people who had incurable diseases and felt hopeless -- the outcasts and the downtrodden. God allowed me to share about my own life and preach from my heart -- telling them about the miracle-working God I served and how he had changed me . . .

The Raven Ministry leaders wanted to start an outreach at a place called the Holland House on West 42nd

Street. An older man and I were asked to lead the Bible studies at that location. Again, I was dumbfounded and amazed that I was chosen to be a part of leading a group. But God says He chooses the weak things of the world to shame the strong; and He uses the foolish to shame the wise. I really began to have a sense that one day God would use me for full time ministry, so I began to prepare my heart to resign my position at GHI.

As with everything in life, God's timing is perfect. As humans, and as sincere as we may be, we often run ahead of God and try to shove the door open. Unfortunately, that's exactly what I did -- I went ahead of God. I decided that it was time for me to be in ministry on a full-time basis and went to my boss Tom, at work and told him that I needed to leave my new job as a Corporate Trainer to go into full time ministry.

Tom was taken aback. Here I was, newly promoted to this position and saying that I needed to quit for full-time ministry. Tom kept asking how I would support my family, but I wouldn't listen to him. Unfortunately, it turns out I wasn't hearing God or my church correctly either. I submitted my resignation, and soon realized that I was only needed once a week for an evening Bible study. By the grace of God, I was given an option to become a part time supervisor for the claims area in the evening. The Bible study was not successful in attracting new believers so we cancelled that outreach. God, however, began to work all things for my good, despite my hasty decisions.

My last assignment, within the training department, was to train a class of college students so they could work part-time hours, in the evening, for the claims operation. Since I wasn't going to do anything further with the Raven Ministry, as I had believed, I was given an opportunity to become the Supervisor for this group of employees. God took my foolish decision and slowly began to turn it into a blessing in disguise! I remained the part-time night supervisor and, ironically, all of the ministry opportunities that opened up through my church were in the evening. I had made all of these changes to join ministry only to end up in a position that wouldn't allow me to. God made sure that in order for me to be a leader in ministry, I needed to learn to be a servant first and I needed to learn how to wait for clear instruction.

One of the many lessons, I learned from this season in my life, was just how gracious God is with His children. Although I realized I had made a mistake regarding the timing of the call of God upon me -- and the fact that I left my full-time position in haste -- I was still able to see God's favor working in my life. The part-time position I had taken was in the claims department—the most central division within the entire company. I was not really qualified to be in that department, let alone in a management position. I was managing a group of college students who came in looking for seasonal and part-time work when they weren't in classes. Since GHI offered paid training, these positions served as an opportunity for college students to work while receiving training that could lead to a future position. Once school started, however, these students would often quit since they already got paid to go through the training class.

The turnover rate was high, and was not a good return on the investment, so I shared my observation with my boss, Mr. Gonzalez. I recommended changing the requirements for these particular training positions; and by speaking up, God allowed me to once again gain favor with the head of my department—like Joseph in the book of Genesis.

Eventually, Mr. Gonzalez began to seek me out more frequently, asking me about my goals, my opinion on certain things and how the job was working out for me. One day, he approached me and said, "Hector, this position is clearly not working out for you. Why don't you come and work directly for me in a full-time day supervisor position that I have available?"

I was intimidated because, although I had been promoted even to the status of a Corporate Trainer for a short time, I knew that the staff members of the claims department at GHI were made up of people who had been working in that department for years. They had experience and they had training. Many were long-term Claims Approvers who had done the work and paid their dues. I knew I couldn't compete with their training, experience, or expertise, and wondered how I could even qualify for a position like that.

The stress surrounding this decision also put my faith in God back into the fire. I ended up taking the job, ultimately choosing to trust God. Mr. Gonzalez made me a roaming supervisor. This position allowed me to be a "floater" to various areas of departmental needs during the week. I worked with claim adjustments, correspondence, and appeals. I worked with the quality assurance team that managed underperforming groups in order to assess the reasons for under-performance, and created solutions to enhance employee performance. I was able to work with various subdivisions within the claims department, learning several aspects of the company in ways I would never have otherwise been exposed to. I learned the entire operation. God was at work in a mysterious place.

Meanwhile, Mr. Gonzalez continued to work very closely with me and groomed me as a supervisor. After about a year or so, I was given a staff of Claims Approvers who processed specialized work for me to supervise. I began to understand, yet again, the depths of God's grace. He was maturing me in my faith by having me engage in work that I was first skeptical and intimidated about doing. God was training me in every area of the claims shop. He managed to take a mistake; I had made, and turn it into a blessing! By setting me up to go to different departments, I was able to learn much in preparation for the future. God, as always, is in control, even though I did not understand the process at the time.

Work was Good, but Everything Else was a Mess

Even as God was continuing to bless me at my work place, my home life with Michelle was challenging and difficult. With both of us working [a decision that I think we would take back and do differently today] and actively involved in church ministry, our kids were shuttled to after-school programs. Amazingly enough, the kids were ok, but family time was strained. There is no doubt that God was the glue that held us all together. He was merciful and blessed us even though; my spiritual life was tottering as well.

Prayer was nowhere to be found. You might say I was going through a dry spell. I was coming to the end of my time with the Raven Ministry and going into a season of sitting in the pews again; and because things had not played out as I had thought they would, I became a little disillusioned with church ministry. I felt like, "What is the point?" Though I still wanted to be used by God and to serve Him, I was questioning if I was really able to do it and if my life would ever amount to anything. In many ways, I adopted an external profession of faith that had no inward reality. Looking back, the only way we made it through those times was by God's grace. He was merciful and faithful to my family and me and carried us each step of the way.

During this challenging season in life, I clung to the promise the Lord showed me in Isaiah 54:4-5 and Vs 13 -15:

"Do not be afraid; you will not suffer shame. Do not fear disgrace; you will not be humiliated. You will forget the shame of your youth and remember no more the reproach of your widowhood. For your Maker is your husband — the LORD Almighty is His name. The LORD will teach all your sons, and great will be your children's peace. In righteousness you will be established: Tyranny will be far from you; you will have nothing to fear. Terror will be far removed; it will not come near you. If anyone does attack you, it will not be my doing; whoever attacks you will surrender to you."

I got involved with a prayer group at work, called Genesis. They met every Wednesday and we all invited fellow employees to come and be a part. Before we knew it, we had twenty people who consistently attended.

During this time, the claims department received a new Senior VP. The new SVP wanted to chart a new course for the company and I soon found out he was a Christian. He heard about our meetings and although he was a top-level executive, and fraternization with lower level folks was not encouraged, it did not deter him from attending the prayer group from time to time. He began coming frequently and union employees, who attended our meetings, were ecstatic that someone in such a high-level position would join.

Every year, the Genesis Group would schedule a church service, followed by a potluck dinner for the group to invite their family and friends to enjoy. That year, they asked me to be the guest preacher.

The group had been trying to find a church space to hold the service, so I connected with a childhood friend who was a member of Calvary Church, a Spanish fellowship on West 47th Street, between 9th and 10th Avenues. I got permission to use the space. It was a place I wanted to stay away from, a place where I had done a lot of my dirt, so to speak. In fact, the irony was that I had been arrested right in front of this church many years before.

As I prepared to preach a sermon to the group, I felt that God wanted me to share my testimony -- every detail. I struggled with this greatly. "Lord, are you sure?" I kept asking Him. At this point, no one in the company really knew anything about my life. They just saw me as Hector Vega, a supervisor in management, part of the prayer group, and a Christian. In fact, some of the people who came to the group worked under my supervisory responsibility.

The day came for the service and potluck. When I got to the church, I saw that the Senior Vice President had come to the meeting and was sitting in the front row. I checked in with God one last time, asking, "Are You sure, Lord, that you want me to share this?"

Did God understand that everyone, as well as a member of the company's leadership, was going to know all about my life? The Lord would not be deterred – I knew I was to press on with my story. My text was in Isaiah 61, which talks about how God gives us beauty for ashes. I told them about my life—that at one point I had even been arrested at the doors of this very church. The Lord allowed me to tell the complete truth, leaving mouths wide open at what God had done in my life. God, ever true to His promises made the service a success! The testimony and the preaching encouraged the people.

The Senior Vice President approached me and said, "You know, Hector, I don't know that I would have done what you did today. It took a lot of courage, and I pray that God blesses you for it."

About a month or so after the event, I was promoted to the position of Department Manager. There were many people who had more education, more training, and more experience than me, but my boss decided I was right for the leadership position.

God had chosen to bless me for doing things His way -- for being honest in my testimony, and for obeying him. I was reminded of the fact that promotion doesn't come from the east or the west, but from the Lord.

...But there were always tests and trials.

A few years after I was promoted to Manager, in 2009, I went on a missionary trip to the land of Egypt (this was not my first mission trip). During this time, my boss, Mr. Gonzalez, was in the process of being promoted. He was asked to make a recommendation regarding who could take his place as director of the department. Mr. Gonzalez suggested me.

While in Egypt, I received an email from Mr. Gonzalez who sternly stated that he had been checking into my work while I was away. He informed me that he found several discrepancies in my work and that he was going to rip the department apart and find someone to fix it.

I didn't bother to respond since I was on the trip and really could not do anything until I got back to work. I determined to just take it all in stride, but suddenly, I got a second email. Mr. Gonzalez wrote to me, stating that I could fix my own errors when I returned as the new Director of the Claims Division.

There is no stopping God! In the sixteen years that I worked with GHI, God continued to move in the company, in the departments, and in my life to bring glory to His name.

CHAPTER 12

A NEW HIGH

Since my early days of preaching in the prison ministry; mission trips; and the Genesis group, the Lord has taken me through a series of events that have been building blocks to His call on my life. I just did not know how and when God would fulfill His plan. One day, God made it clear it was time to begin stepping into alignment with His will for me to be in ministry.

And it all began with a dream . . .

A Dream

In January 2002 Pastor Carter Conlon, of Times Square Church, called the church to a three-day fast. On the second day of the fast, I had a dream.

In the dream, I was in front of Times Square Church, standing with Max, the leader of the Raven Ministry. Max stepped into the church, and Pastor Carter approached and asked me if I had seen Max. I told him he had just gone inside. Then Pastor Carter looked at me and asked, "How are you doing?" I replied, "I'm doing okay."

He took his right hand, tapped me on the shoulder and said, "Get ready to preach."

I stood there stunned, not knowing what to say. He went inside, and I went inside right behind him. It was an evening service, and Pastor Carter went up to the stage and announced that there would be a guest speaker that night: Hector Vega.

I don't remember speaking in the dream because a couple of people rose up in the pews, and there was commotion over the fact that Pastor Carter had invited me to preach. In fact, some in the crowd were protesting because there had been so many others who were more qualified to speak. I was puzzled by it all and somehow sensed that some were not happy because they felt they had attended Times Square Church longer, or were better qualified to speak. I mean, who was I? I remember turning to the pastor and saying, "I can return at another time if you want?" The scene in the dream shifted and I was now being asked to come up to the 4th floor to meet Pastor Carter for an assignment of sorts. I awoke and shared this peculiar dream with Michelle. She hated that I woke her up early, but I had to tell someone about this dream.

My first step in fulfilling God's call in my life that year was to go out into the world and serve, on the mission field, with members of the church. I went on my first mission's trip with Times Square Church, to Mexico. During the first or second day of the trip, we went into a town where Pastor Rick Hagan [a pastor from Harvest Evangelism who led the teams] had been ministering, and had gathered people from all over the neighborhood.

Pastor Rick called me over and said, "Hector, I want you to get people to testify and have them participate in worship. I want you to preach in Spanish."

Because of the dream I had, I had been motivated to spend more time sitting at God's feet—studying the Word of God and praying—and preparing messages that the Lord began to give me. I had remained in deep study of the Bible, for a period of time, in order to write the sermons that God was placing on my heart to share with others.

The first night the Lord gave me a message and several people responded to the altar call. A man from Alabama, Roy Busby, said, "I don't know what you said, but I almost went up there just to make sure I was saved." You look like the 'Banty' Rooster up there. His words really encouraged me and confirmed that the Lord had spoken through me.

That week, Pastor Rick took me under his wing and told me how the Lord speaks to Him in preparing his messages. He taught me that I needed to be pliable and ready—that I had a calling on my life to preach. In fact, Pastor Rick confirmed the many things the Lord had already spoken to me.

Nigeria

Later that same year, I was to go on a missions' trip to Nigeria. As was customary at Times Square Church, those desiring to go on a trip would first be interviewed by the missions department. There were two women who interviewed me.

One of the women, Fayette, asked, "What do you think your gifts and callings are?"

I paused for a moment, and then said, "I believe God is calling me to preach."

Fayette frowned, as she looked me over. "Well, I don't think you're going to have an opportunity to do that on this trip," she said.

I responded, "I am not going to Nigeria to preach. I am going to serve and to ask God to be glorified in my life." She smiled and said, "I am just letting you know because people often come with hidden agendas." I completely understood and appreciated Fayette's candidness.

We arrived in Jos, Nigeria, and about forty of us went into a prison to minister to the inmates. As our medical team ministered to the inmates' physical needs, the rest of us went into the chapel to participate in the church service. There were over a hundred inmates in the little chapel.

Fayette was on our team and came to me in a panic. "Do you know where Glenda is?" she asked.

I said, "No. Is there a problem?"

"We don't have anyone to preach!" she answered. After a moment, she looked at me and said, "Hey! Do you think you could preach a message?"

We both smiled at each other – knowing the irony that in spite of everything, God made a way for me to preach during this mission trip. It was yet another reminder that God is *always* in control.

I spoke for about five minutes on the Gospel of Jesus Christ. I remember thinking that it wasn't a very eloquent message. Actually, I really thought I blew it. I sat back down after the brief comments and short message, and people were looking at each other wondering what was going on. They asked me to come back up and do an altar call. My altar call was simply, "Does anybody want Jesus?"

To my surprise, many came forward to respond and to give their lives for the One who gave himself for them.

Since that time, I have had the privilege of traveling all over the world to share the good news about our loving Savior. I have been to Burundi, Greece, Cuba, Morocco, Argentina, India, Egypt, Switzerland, France and Colombia. Most of these trips have been edifying, in the sense that they allowed me the opportunity to develop and grow as a Christian first, and as a person training for the ministry second. I have been blessed by each of these trips. There are many stories and signposts of faith that God weaved into each trip. At every stop, there were things that solidified my faith for the future.

Molding a Vessel for His Use

As I mentioned earlier, it is written in 1 Corinthians 1:27 that God often uses "the foolish things of this world to confound the wise." In the prior verse, it says, "Brothers, think of what you were when you were called. Not many of you were wise by human standards; not many were influential; not many were of noble birth."

God often takes the least likely – the nobodies – and uses them in tremendous ways. That is essentially what the Lord chosen to do with me. I am a living testimony of the power of God to do what most of us would say is unthinkable.

In late 2007, Times Square Church started a small class called MIP—(Ministers Internship Program). I don't know all of the specifics on why they started this, but it was a Godsend for me. The Lord placed me in a class with one of the Times Square Church pastoral staff members, Pastor William Carroll, who has ever since been a mentor to me. As I participated in the class, I was in awe – and I was humbled by the fact that there were so many people who I looked up to, many who were technically more qualified than I was to be a minister. There were people who were more educated than me; people that had done far fewer bad things in their life; and people who had been serving longer in the church and in ministry. But the Lord saw fit to once again to open a door for me. The class was not an invitation for people to come and become a pastor, nor was it an invitation for preachers to learn to preach. It was an invitation to come, sit, and listen. It was a time to get to know Jesus in a different way; to let God do whatever He wanted. Our role was to attend the class and learn how to read the Bible a little differently. There were no diplomas or promises of any position.

Instinctively I knew I was exactly where God wanted me to be. The class topics began to challenge me as "iron sharpens iron". I also got an opportunity to develop more friendships with some of the people in the class. These friends would prove essential and fruitful for the future ministry that God had planned.

The Significance of Melia, Morocco

In 2008, Michelle and I decided to visit a friend of mine named Cesar. Years earlier, we had met Cesar on a mission trip to Cuba, where he traveled often to minister. During one of the trips back to the states, he felt led to this little place called Melia. He left his job and apartment, and moved to Morocco where God began to do miraculous things. By the time we arrived, he had three separate congregations meeting in his church: Spanish, Muslims converting to Jesus, and refugees from Sudan. We had a wonderful trip. We saw the land, saw the work, and loved the people of Morocco.

A strange thing happened upon our return home. Michelle and I went to Times Square Church, as we normally did, to attend Tuesday night service. As soon as we arrived, a strange feeling came over me. At first I couldn't really identify what was going on. Times Square Church was my church home and the people were my church family. Still, I felt out-of-sorts.

I turned to Michelle and asked, "Are you having the same feeling I'm having?"

She gave me a look and said, "Why? What type of feeling are you having?"

I couldn't quite put my finger on it. Finally I answered, "It almost feels like...like we're just here visiting instead of attending our own church."

Michelle agreed with me.

Neither one of us could figure out why we suddenly felt like we were visitors at our home church.

Several weeks after that, I received a phone call from Pastor Cesar, asking me if I could travel back to Morocco to cover for him in his church. He had been asked to speak to Muslim missionaries on techniques to reach the Muslim people. Pastor Cesar wanted me to lead the church, as a substitute pastor, while he traveled to the conference. I had never heard of such a thing. In fact, the only memories I had of substitutes were teachers; and they never turned out well. Furthermore, I wasn't a pastor and had never even considered serving in that capacity. Preaching a message and being a pastor are two different callings. The thought of being responsible for the spiritual life of people was huge. Yet, after receiving permission from my ministry leaders, I went to Morocco and helped out Pastor Cesar and thanked God that nothing disastrous took place.

Soon after I returned from Morocco, I was asked to share a testimony with the Prison Ministry at Times Square Church, in which I had been serving for quite some time. I shared a little about my life and some of the recent things the Lord had been using me to do. One of the last things I shared was about how I had been given the opportunity to serve in the role of substitute pastor in Morocco. I made it clear to the team that I had no desires or hopes to be a pastor and could never see myself becoming one. The realities and weight of the position had become clearer to me and I now saw Pastor Carter Conlon in a new light. Pastor Carter's job was safe from me!

What in the World is God thinking?

In January of 2009, the same year I was promoted to Director of Claims operation, the Times Square Church Missions Department asked me to lead a small team to Egypt, to minister the Word of God to the Egyptian people. In preparation for the mission's trip, we were asked to attend a service at East Harlem Fellowship to minister to a small congregation. It was in Harlem that I first met Senior Pastor, Ivan Rios. We had a good discussion and seemed to hit it off well. The church met in a small basement space of a building. There was no glamour, nor bells or whistles. A few weeks went by and I received a call from Pastor Ivan asking me to return as a guest preacher on Easter Sunday.

I once again felt a sense of panic because Easter is a big day in the church calendar, and it was already the afternoon of Ash Wednesday. Somehow, however, I felt that I had to say yes and preach on Easter. So, I returned to preach at the East Harlem Fellowship. Following that Easter Sunday, later that week, I received a call for a meeting with Treg McCoy, the Missions Director at Times Square Church, and Pastor Ivan.

Treg told me that Pastor Ivan was stepping down and it had been decided by Times Square Church leadership that I should be appointed as the pastor of the East Harlem Fellowship Church. I was numb at first, trying to comprehend what was being asked of me. I also thought to myself, how did you get my name for this position, I didn't apply and my resume is not that great -- they must be smoking something. I felt gratitude for being considered for such a role, but there was also fear. My mind raced. How could I do this? I never went to seminary. What would I do? I mean I just told people in the Prison ministry this was not what I wanted to do in life. After all, pastoring is not like being an evangelist. You have to preach every Sunday and mid week service to the same people and I only had 2 sermons in my briefcase. What in the world would I do with the other 50 weeks! I explained to Treg that I would need to pray about it and discuss it with Michelle because I knew it was a calling for the entire family. It was a call for us all to lay down our lives. It would call for sacrifice on a family level.

That moment also brought me a sense of awe, since God is the One who puts people in certain positions. Most awesome of all, I had not applied for the pastoral position at East Harlem Fellowship. I wasn't even aware the position would become vacant. It was totally the Lord who was appointing me, deciding the time, and the place. That night we had a Vega family meeting where my kids were asked if I should do this. My oldest son Nicholas shrugged, "I don't know" when I asked should I do it. My middle son, Josiah, blurted out, "No dad don't do it! I don't want to be a pastor's kid. I don't want people expecting me to act a certain way and I don't want to leave Times Square church." Finally my youngest, Seth, said, "Do it Dad."

After prayer and deliberation, Michelle and I made the decision to accept God's call. I became the pastor at East Harlem Fellowship. Pastor Ivan made the announcement to the congregation during the Mother's Day Service in 2009 and I have been the pastor of that church to this day.

The next Sunday we had an encounter with some NYC rats in the church space and I said to myself, "What was I thinking when I said yes to this?"

The Fruit of Obedience

Ever since I made the decision to obey the calling that God placed on my life -- to become the pastor of East

Harlem Fellowship -- I have seen Him do the miraculous in the congregation He is building and in my life as well.

There have been countless miracles that have occurred since the Lord grabbed hold of my heart and transformed my life all those years ago. And though the process has not been easy, my life and Michelle's life has served as a testimony to the power of God – and that no one, and I do mean *no one*, is beyond God's reach.

Today, East Harlem Fellowship is a growing congregation offering numerous services for everyone. With a congregation made up of people with very diverse social economic and cultural backgrounds, East Harlem Fellowship has a bright future with many goals for reaching deeper into the community and serving at a more powerful level.

Michelle and I lead the church, that is serving the East Harlem community through outreaches including the coffee house ministry, "Café con Leche", the street evangelism team, the high school mentors club in a public high school, and events like Freedom Fest and Rock the Block, a loud and boisterous street party that proclaims Christ as Lord and Savior through music, food, and face painting. We have begun to support global communities through our own mission's trips, sending teams into countries such as Greece, The Philippines, Morocco, Cuba and Puerto Rico.

Although East Harlem Fellowship has continued to work with its parent congregation, Times Square Church,

God has done miracles to ensure that the rapidly growing congregation in Harlem can grow on its own.

In January 2013, responding to the growing congregation, the Lord provided a larger church facility. In yet another ironic twist, that only God can make possible, we have recently been given favor to minister to the local police department through appreciation banquets. Who would have ever thought Hector Vega would be ministering to the police department? One day I was asked to share at a police roll call meeting. Can you believe that? Only God!

It has been a blessing to watch what the Lord has done in my life, the lives of my family members and within the church in which I serve.

CHAPTER 13

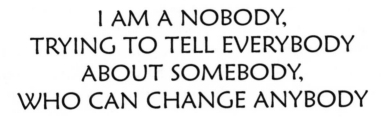

I AM A NOBODY, TRYING TO TELL EVERYBODY ABOUT SOMEBODY, WHO CAN CHANGE ANYBODY

You did not choose me but I chose you and appointed you to go and bear fruit. And that your fruit should remain.

—John 15:16

April 3, 2016 – Ordination Day – 7 years in the making and ironically happening during the Jewish year of Jubilee.

I am standing at the pulpit of Times Square Church, the place where some of the best preachers in the world have stood and preached. It's a sobering moment and surreal. All at once a million thoughts run through my mind.

The improbability of my standing there is overwhelming when so many years before this day I entered the doors of this church, broken, strung out and without hope.

I was reminded of a day in the early 90's when I sat in the balcony with my girlfriend, Michelle. I remember hearing the sermon and sensing that the preacher seemed to have an ability to hear and speak with God. Perhaps he could speak to God on my behalf and get the court case that was hanging over me, dismissed. This seemed like a great idea to me! I mean some go to the witch doctor, why shouldn't I go to the preacher? I've got nothing to lose.

His name was Pastor David Wilkerson, and his sermons in those days were still very much fire and brimstone, but I was moved. I mentioned to Michelle that I wanted to go back stage and ask for prayer. She told me that due to security measures I would not be allowed back stage. I said "Don't you worry, I know how to get through stuff." I made it to Pastor Dave and asked him to pray for me so that the open court case on drugs would get dismissed. He looked at me with the (prophet) eyes that seemed to look right through me and see my thoughts. He said, "Son, are you looking for Jesus with all your heart"? I paused and quickly responded. "Jesus, no I am here for the case and to get it dismissed." He looked at me as if he knew something I didn't. "Son, if you are not looking for Jesus, then I am not agreeing with that prayer. I will pray that Jesus gets a hold of your heart and you serve Him". I left dumbfounded and mumbled as I walked away. What kind of a church is this? They won't even pray for you, but the encounter would eventually signal to me that Jesus was serious business and not a witch doctor or anything I was accustomed to.

So here I stand, looking out over the crowd numbering a couple thousand, waiting to hear me share a little bit of my journey with God. I am nervous and my mouth becomes dry. I remember the mistakes along the way, but also the successes and the times God rescued me from the pit. The emotions rush in and overwhelm my composure, but I fight it.

Instinctively I know that I am at a new fork in the road, a crossroad. The road before me will get a little narrower. I sense a voice in my spirit saying come up higher and go in deeper.

As Pastor Carter gets up to challenge me, pray for me and speak words over me, he says, "It's ironic: here is an ex cop ordaining an ex convict. Only God can do this!"

I am charged to seek the leadership and empowerment of the Holy Spirit, as I will need the strength of God more than ever. I am charged

*to practice the Word of God and let my life become
a living demonstration of it.*

*I hear, in his words, the confirmation of what
I am sensing; I am no longer called to civilian
affairs, the business world, etc. I am strictly
charged to be a preacher and pastor and give
myself sacrificially and wholeheartedly to the
work of God, His leading and His provision.*

Looking out on the miraculous power of God, I
have to say that if He had done nothing more than to get
me clean and sober, it would have still been much more
than I deserved. If He had simply decided to heal me from
the rampant drug abuse and give me the gift of salvation,
it would have been more than enough.

But He didn't stop there.

He has given me my family. I have an awesome,
Godly wife and three awesome sons. In fact, as I write
this, Michelle and I have celebrated 23 years of marriage.
And lest you think that God saved me, cleaned me up,
and everyone lived happily ever after – I still struggle with
feelings of inadequacy as a husband, father, and Pastor.
As long as we have breath in this world, there will always
be trials and ups and downs in life. The enemy of our
souls doesn't give up trying to discourage or sidetrack
God's children. But, that comes with being an heir to the
King. As long as you have God in your life, no matter the

hardship, trial or circumstance, you will not go down in flames. The Lord uses difficulties to mold us into the men and women He wants us to be. Nothing is wasted when it comes to God working in our lives. One of my favorite childhood sayings is, "If you are in the schoolyard and the bully looks like he is going to take you down, you better go down swinging. Don't you dare come home without putting up a fight."

It's beyond comprehension that He chose to trust me to stand as His representative and teach His Word to the people. He chose me to lead His people to grow in their faith, to serve Him in their daily walk and to serve others through His love. I am chosen to be one example of who God is and what He represents on the earth. I am one of the people God has chosen to help safeguard His most prized possession—His Church, His Bride, the apple of His eye.

Even as a pastor, things can get rough. It can be a lonely life no matter how many people are around you. Sometimes I look at the people I am leading, and look for clues in their walk that my service to God, and His ministry, is actually producing fruit. Sometimes all I see is the daily struggle. Have you ever felt that way? Of course you have – we all do; rich or poor, educated or uneducated, people of all colors and families of origin. It's in times of struggle that we can forge ahead, knowing that our work for the Lord is never in vain.

So often we don't see the fruit played out in front of us because it's being played out in people's hearts. I am telling you this because it's important to understand that our lives as Christians are not easy, but, the road we travel is definitely blessed. And we serve God because we *want* to serve Him, not because we want to gain glory in this life and not because of the blessings, but because he is worthy. God will keep us humble – especially those He has called to full-time ministry. And that is a good thing. Humility protects us from our sinful selves and ensures the spiritual welfare of those who look to us for guidance.

The Lord has changed and transformed me from being a miserable drug addict to a man of God – a flawed man of God, but a man of God just the same. I am guaranteed that EVERYTHING that happens in my life will work out for good – God will use it all to mold me into the man He wants me to be, and to allow me the honor to help bring about His glory.

He chose me! I still have trouble processing it. What amazes me the most about our awesome, merciful God is that even after all of this--after all He has done—dying on the cross for my sins, saving me from my drug abuse, giving me my family, career, and ministry—He continues to do the miraculous. He continues to write chapters in my life.

In 2015, I was selected to lead a homeless mission in Newark, New Jersey, near where I first joined the Genesis Program. The ministry had been experiencing some challenges and needed some stability. I was named the Executive Director/CEO of this fine ministry called *Goodwill Rescue Mission*. It's been a Christian mission for 120 years. I am responsible for the personal, professional, and spiritual development of 20 employees; the financial solvency and integrity of the mission; the development of strategic and collaborative partnerships with businesses and other community non-profits; and to ensure that the men, in our life transformation program, meet expected outcomes, milestones for success, and become productive members of society -- restored to their families and independent living.

We serve over 225 meals a day to men, women, and children. We shelter up to 43 men every night, and in the winter the numbers can grow to 80 per night. Every night we hold chapel service where the broken can find strength, encouragement, and hope in Jesus.

It's amazing -- I never thought I would be alive, let alone doing this work. But as it says in the Apostle Paul's letter to the Ephesians (3:20-21): *"Now to Him who is able to do exceedingly abundantly above all that we ask or think, according to the power that works in us, to Him be glory in the church by Christ Jesus to all generations, forever and ever. Amen."*

What Jesus Christ has done for me, He can do for YOU! Are you ready to live a different life – the *good* life? Please pray with me right where you are. The Word of God says that whoever calls upon the name of the Lord shall be saved.

You may be asking, "What am I being saved from?"

I know some of you reading this book feel broken and that life has passed you by. You may feel like you have reached the point of no return. Your life feels like a tangled mess that can never be untangled. But, I am a living testimony that it's not too late to make a change – your hope is in God because He is able to straighten out the crooked mess that is your life. Perhaps you can acknowledge that you sense a deep longing -- a void in your life that has never been satisfied with drugs, clubs, men, women, money, etc. Maybe you are successful in life; you have achieved status, financial independence, and enjoy the perfect career, and yet, you still feel woefully inadequate and unfulfilled.

Perhaps you, like me, can be honest and say, "I have caused a lot of pain to a lot of people over the years and have done things I'm not proud of -- things I would love to make amends for, or forget." There are some reading this book, that have not experienced drug abuse, or any of the issues I struggled with and wrote about, but you have nonetheless, felt the sting of life without a relationship with the Living God. You have carried the weight of living without purpose or meaning.

Friend, what is your prison? Is it drugs, alcohol, anger, sex, pornography, fear, un-forgiveness, bitterness? Is it the feeling that you will never measure up; the feeling that no one likes the real you? Oh, I serve a God who can open every prison door; He can shine a light in every prison cell and show you the way out.

Do you wonder if you can ever be forgiven? Do you desire to come to a place in life where you can just start again? There is good news for you – you *can be* forgiven; you *can start* again. Jesus Christ died to set you free. He wants to transform you; renew your mind; and give you a new life – an abundant life, both now and forever.

Do you want to turn your life over to God? Do you want to accept Jesus into your heart so that He becomes not only your Savior, but your Lord as well?

Let us pray together.

"Lord Jesus, today I recognize my failures, my sense of being lost and my lack of purpose. I recognize that I have done things that are not right – that are sinful and against Your perfect law. I believe that You died on a cross because You were and are the Lamb of God who takes away the sin of the world. Your name is Jesus because You will save Your people from their sins. I accept Your free gift of salvation and believe that You died to secure my righteousness, for forgiveness for my sins, and for my peace that surpasses any peace this world can give. I receive Your gift by faith. I give You permission to enter my life; to lead and guide me from this day forward. I want to know You personally. I don't understand it all, but I want to believe and walk with you. Help me, Lord; cleanse me, empower me, save me, heal me, and deliver me from my doubts and despair. Show me the way home. I pray these things in the name of Jesus, Amen."

Hallelujah!

My friend, I encourage you to find a Bible-believing church and become an active part of that fellowship. It will help you to grow in your walk with God, serve the Lord, and live for Him first and foremost. You will never regret it.

And then please share your story.

Go to www.eastharlemfellowship.org or send me an email at eastharlemfellowship@gmail.com and receive prayer, resources, and support for your new walk with God.

Welcome to your new family; the family of God.

EPILOGUE

RESCUED TO RESCUE

God rescued me for a reason. He rescued me through His divine intervention and through the lives of many people who loved and cared about me. Those who had been rescued themselves, who had came to know the love, grace, and mercy of Jesus Christ and the Power found in the good news message (THE GOSPEL).

The Lord tells us in his word that "he who is forgiven much, loves much" and to "him that is given much, much is required." It's been nearly three years since the last chapter of this book and the writing of this Epilogue. I think we can all agree that I have been given much! In this season of my life, I am not satisfied with just attending church on Sunday. I am not satisfied with preaching a 3-point sermon, patting myself on the back and then going home to enjoy the baseball or football game. I am not satisfied (or interested in) pursuing a corporate salary, fancy house, nice car, or endless vacations. In fact, I'm not satisfied with receiving a salary for doing something (pastoring a church) that I was willing to do for free out of a heart of gratitude.

Instead, I feel a burden, a responsibility to pass a lit torch. I believe there are too many of us enjoying the blessings of salvation without taking risks to bring the message of freedom to those who need it most.

I heard that during the tragedy of the Titanic the nearest ship was just miles away, but it was off duty. It could have rescued all the passengers if it were on duty! In the same way, many Christians are "off duty," while so many hurting, destitute, and lost people need rescuing. Just as I was rescued through God's mercy and grace, I want to lead an army of normal Christians who truly make a difference in the lives of our neighbors.

At East Harlem Fellowship, we continue to immerse ourselves in what it means to Love God, Love People and Be the Church in a practical way. All throughout history, the people who walked closely with God were often sent into difficult places to be a light, a testimony of faith and hope. They were sent to be the solution to the problems in their neighborhood and to leave a legacy for future generations. We are living in a time where it seems our walls, lives and churches are broken down. The testimony of the people of God and there public influence is weak again in the land. We believe the people of God "the church" has to be a transforming agent outside the four walls of the temple. This was the model of the first century church. They turned their communities upside down for God and for Good. We hear a lot of talk about the gospel having power to change. But I believe the full gospel has implications beyond proclaiming the message of salvation and spiritual formation of disciples. Those who proclaim and carry the full gospel should demonstrate compassion, relieve oppression, alleviate poverty, and restore individuals and communities to wholeness, as we partner with the Holy Spirit. We want to see spiritual justice come back to the public square once again.

God wants our faith to reflect His Son, Jesus Christ, both in our personal lives. Ask yourself, are we making a difference in our homes, in our communities, in our nation, and in our world? On the practical side, are we making a difference on the streets where real life occurs on a day by day basis?

Jesus didn't stay within the walls of the Temple, He walked the streets, went to the neighborhoods, and to the people that the religious leaders avoided and even hated. Jesus wasn't afraid to face any obstacle to be with the poor and the spiritual outcast. His mission was to set the captives free. Is that our mission? He reached out to them, He ate with them, and He healed them – because He loved them. In fact, He loved them so much, that He died for them.

This is the passion that the Lord wants burning in our hearts – a passion for people. Please do not misunderstand me, the fire I feel is not at all tied to me or you "doing" more stuff. In fact, for the first time in my life, I am learning about the value of resting in the finished work of what Jesus did for me instead of what I can do for him.

No, I'm not talking about "busyness" and "programs" for the sake of programs; instead, I'm talking about believers having the heart of Christ for people who need to be rescued from sin and despair. I'm talking about allowing the power of God, the light of heaven, to touch the darkness around us.

So let me ask you, are you willing to show the same grace, mercy and love to someone that God has shown to you? Are you ready to rise above the comfort of your salvation and live a more courageous Christian life – a life that is devoted to rescuing others in the same way that God rescued you?

God has saved you not to just give you a free ticket to eternal life, but to work through you to love others and bring them into His kingdom.

Pray and seek the Lord's will – "What would you have me to do; whom do you want me to be" and the Lord will lead you into a bold and courageous walk of faith.

Give me this mountain . . .

Joshua 14:10-12 says,

"And now, behold, the Lord has kept me alive, as He said, these forty-five years, ever since the Lord spoke this word to Moses while Israel wandered in the wilderness; and now, here I am this day, eighty-five years old. As yet I am as strong this day as on the day that Moses sent me; just as my strength was then, so now is my strength for

war, both for going out and for coming in. Now therefore, give me this mountain of which the Lord spoke in that day; for you heard in that day how the Anakim were there, and that the cities were great and fortified. It may be that the Lord will be with me, and I shall be able to drive them out as the Lord said."

As I sit here today thinking about my life, the words of Caleb come to mind and all I can say is WOW GOD. What He has done in my life is no different than what he wants to do in your life. No, the path is not all roses – I have been blessed for sure, but there have also been pit stops, detours, times of confusion, walls of silence, and even seasons of doubt. The path of faith includes real life experiences and difficulties, but it also includes God's sovereign hand that guides us, molds us, and shapes us into the people He wants us to be. It's a journey that is walked hand in hand with the Lord and one that provides peace, comfort and victory in the midst of our circumstances.

At this point in my faith, the Lord is stirring me to ask for the mountain! My heart and vision is to see the church I lead become all that God would have us to be in our community (mission field); meaning, very simply, that we would be willing to live as Christians on a mission.

The mountain that I am asking God for is not just for my local church, but also for us to be part of a movement who do not settle for defeat or less than what God has for us. My heart's cry and passion is that we would throw off everything that is hindering our profession of faith, sapping our power to overcome, and rendering us as useless. My hope is to raise up mission-minded Christians, who are equipped and passionate about being the church; who see the world as a battlefield and not a playground. I want to see the power of God unleashed in my generation. I want to see that the only measure of success in churches is a transformed life impacting other lives and not the amount of people attending church on Sunday.

What does this vision look like in a practical sense? Honestly its too big to articulate. It's being used by God to be a rescuer, an advocate for drug addicts; ex- offenders reentering society; youth who are unmotivated, depressed, hopeless, and without role models; single moms and children who are impoverished, alone, or within domestic violence shelters that need hope and a home; people who have given up or who see no way out of their circumstances; and every neighbor that needs the love, compassion, and mercy of Christ. My passion is for the church to share the Gospel and to BE a reflection of Jesus as we come alongside all of our "neighbors." One Life at a time!

There is no Plan B. We are the solution for our community because God is with us.

The church I pastor, East Harlem Fellowship is a multicultural, multigenerational, Evangelical church and international outreach located in the heart of East Harlem. We are preparing to launch into this vision that I have shared and what we believe is our promise land journey (The Way Out)! In fact, our vision includes a Ministry Facility that will offer, not only spiritual help, but tangible physical help as well.

We encourage you to join us in this vision. No matter where you fellowship or where you live, you too can be a part of this movement! Remember, as Christians, we have a unique responsibility to put love into action as we care for those around us for the sake of the Gospel. We have all been given a mandate to love God, love people.

Because the Lord gave his all, we are called to do the same and leave a legacy of generosity. We believe that as we act on this, we will see our communities thrive. We will witness our neighbors grow in faith and grace and our families will be touched with peace and heavenly blessing. Our own lives will be changed too as we live for the glory of God and the souls of men and women.

Will you join us in this effort?

There are many ways you can be involved in this movement – whether it's in person, through social media, or working with us to impact YOUR community!

I invite you to go to the following contact page to connect and engage with us! And while you are at it, let me know how the Lord has worked in your life and where you sense Him leading you now.

May we all unite together to be the church that God can work through at this special time in history and at this special hour...

WE WANT TO HEAR FROM YOU!

Hector Vega's gripping story, *Arrested by Grace*, is being shared around the world as a story of hope and healing. Do you have a similar story? Have you overcome drug addiction, imprisonment, or maybe other hidden struggles - abuse, failure, loneliness, depression, anxiety, or rejection? Hector would love to hear from you. Share your story of hope and healing at www.ArrestedByGrace.org.

Also, if the book has been an encouragement to you, or made an impact in your life, please share with us. If you would like to have Hector Vega speak at your event, please complete the event form on the website.

CPSIA information can be obtained
at www.ICGtesting.com
Printed in the USA
FFHW012123200519
52387959-58035FF